Department 56®
Villages

The Heritage Village Collection®

Dickens' Village • New England Village • Alpine Village
Christmas in the City • North Pole • Disney Parks Village Series

The Original Snow Village®

Secondary Market Price Guide
& Collector Handbook

SECOND EDITION

Dickens' Village Mill
The Heritage Village Collection
Secondary Market Value: $5,080

Cathedral Church
The Original Snow Village
Secondary Market Value: $2,540

The most valuable retired pieces in Heritage Village and Snow Village:
"Dickens' Village Mill" (#6519-6) and "Cathedral Church" (#5067-4)

Department 56®
Villages

To Joe . . . Wow! Talent, tenacity, technology . . . thanks, thanks, thanks.

Special thanks for their assistance in the photography of pieces; New England House of Collectibles – Meriden, CT; G & L Christmas Barn – Windham, CT; Periwinkle – Vernon, CT; Jeff & Susan McDermott; Dan & Claire Kavanagh

This publication is *not* affiliated with Department 56,® Inc. or any of its affiliates, subsidiaries, distributors or representatives. Any opinions expressed are solely those of the authors, and do not necessarily reflect those of Department 56,® Inc. The Heritage Village Collection®, The Original Snow Village®, Dickens' Village®, New England Village® and Christmas in the City® are registered trademarks of Department 56,® Inc. Alpine Village©, North Pole©, Disney Parks Village Series©, Little Town of Bethlehem©, Charles Dickens' Signature Series© and the American Architecture Series© are copyrights of Department 56. Product names and product designs are the property of Department 56,® Inc., Eden Prairie, MN. Photographs by Collectors' Publishing Co., Inc.

Front cover (left to right): "Dickens' Village Mill," *Dickens' Village*; "Route 1, North Pole, Home of Mr. & Mrs. Claus," *North Pole*; "Town Church," *The Original Snow Village*.
Back cover (top to bottom): "Seven Swans-A-Swimming," *Dickens' Village (accessory)*; "Santa's Workshop," *North Pole*; "J. Hudson Stoveworks," *New England Village*; "Cathedral Church" (#5067-4), *The Original Snow Village*; "Norman Church," *Dickens' Village*.

Managing Editor:	Jeff Mahony	Art Director:	Joe T. Nguyen
Associate Editor:	Mike Micciulla	Staff Artist:	Scott Sierakowski
Editorial Assistants:	Gia C. Manalio		
	Katie M. Adams		

ISBN 1-888914-04-1

Collectors' Publishing Co., Inc.
598 Pomeroy Avenue
Meriden, CT 06450
http://www.collectorspub.com

CONTENTS

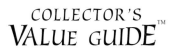

COLLECTOR'S
VALUE GUIDE™

CONTENTS

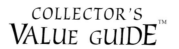

COLLECTOR'S
VALUE GUIDE™

Introducing The Collector's Value Guide™

Welcome to the second edition of the Department 56 Villages Collector's Value Guide, which is now in full color! Collectors already love our easy-to-use alphabetical listings and color-coded tabs and the brilliant new color photos make it even easier to identify the pieces in your collection. The Collector's Value Guide is designed to answer any questions you have about your collection:

- What are the secondary market values of my pieces?

- What are the new pieces this year and which are retiring?

- How many pieces do I have and which variations do I own?

- What is my own collection really worth?

This is what the value guide is all about – bringing you everything you need to know about The Heritage Village Collection and The Original Snow Village, and all in one volume. Inside these pages, you will find a wealth of information about new releases, the ins and outs of the secondary market, display ideas, information on variations of pieces and much more.

Best of all, the value guide lists every building and accessory in Heritage Village and Snow Village, along with their secondary market values. The value guide is designed so that you can fill in the market price of your pieces, which will tell you exactly what your own collection is worth. These values have been gathered from a wide range of sources from all over the country, and are an accurate benchmark that collectors can use to price their pieces for resale, for insurance purposes or just for fun. Other helpful features of the value guide include a glossary of collecting terms, two easy-to-use indexes (alphabetical and numerical) and a "Collectors' Notebook" section for jotting down important addresses, dates or general notes about collecting. Whether you're a collector who's been enchanted by the rich fantasy of The Heritage Village Collection or enamored with the 1950s nostalgia of The Original Snow Village, the easy-to-use Collector's Value Guide makes collecting more fun than ever!

COLLECTOR'S
VALUE GUIDE™

Heritage Village Overview

The Heritage Village Collection is a world of rich tradition and bustling activity, of tree-lined country roads, sloping hills and city splendor. There are six distinctive villages within the Heritage Village Collection as well as the Little Town of Bethlehem nativity set.

Dickens' Village®

Since its introduction in 1984, *Dickens' Village* has been the most popular series in The Heritage Village Collection. Inspired by the author Charles Dickens and the Victorian era in which he lived, *Dickens' Village* brings the magic of 19th century London to thousands of devoted collectors in an ever-growing collection of shops, pubs, churches, mills and cottages. The detailed buildings and delightful accessories bring the essence of Victorian London to life; you can almost hear the clip-clop of carriage horses trotting down cobblestone streets, smell the aroma of fresh-baked Christmas puddings or feel the prickly coarseness of a thatched roof.

There have been 99 lighted buildings issued in *Dickens' Village* to date and 29 are currently available. Every facet of Victorian English life is represented in the collection, from the bustle of small, family-run shops to the grand pageantry of the British aristocracy (reflected in recent pieces like "Dursley Manor" and the "Ramsford Palace" limited edition set).

Among the authentic era pieces are several buildings and accessories that have been based on fictional characters and locations in various Dickens novels, including *A Christmas Carol*, *The Old Curiosity Shop*, *Nicholas Nickleby*, *David Copperfield* and *Oliver Twist*. Fans of the author will be delighted by the latest piece in the *Charles Dickens' Signature Series*, "Gad's Hill Place," which is based on the house in which Charles Dickens actually lived.

COLLECTOR'S
VALUE GUIDE™

New England Village®

If you've ever wished you could step into a Currier & Ives Christmas card, you'll appreciate *New England Village*, with its white clapboard churches, simple frame houses, lighthouses and covered bridges. The series debuted in 1986 with a set of seven buildings which created a perfect small-town New England scene with a town hall, a schoolhouse, a general store and more. Like every small town, growth is inevitable and the collection has expanded to include 46 individual lighted buildings with 15 currently available.

The great diversity of this village allows you to create your own vision of New England. With several farmhouses and barns to choose from, you can create part of your *New England Village* as a farming community. The various shops, private homes and churches can create a close-knit, hardworking hamlet where everyone's on a first name basis or you can create a coastal village display when you add the new "Navigational Charts & Maps" to "Pierce Boat Works" (1995) and "Cape Keag Fish Cannery" (1994). The distinctive geography of New England means you can have snow-capped mountains, vast green forests, pastoral fields and tranquil streams, all in the same village display.

Alpine Village©

Nestled among the snowy mountain ridges of the German, Austrian and Swiss Alps, Department 56's *Alpine Village* is a exotic *wünder*-land of winter delights. Collectors of *Alpine Village* can can close their eyes and imagine the sweet smell of chocolate wafting from the "Bakery & Chocolate Shop" (1994), the crisp sound of skis cutting through virgin snow near the ski lodge, "Kamm Haus" (1995), and the deep resonance of an alpenhorn echoing from the newest building release, "Danube Music Publisher." Issued in 1986, the original five-piece set of *Alpine Village* consisted of a restaurant and various merchant shops, but the village has since grown to include churches, a grist mill, a train station and more. The collection now includes 16 lighted buildings and 11 of the buildings are currently available.

COLLECTOR'S
VALUE GUIDE™

Heritage Village Overview

Christmas in the City®

    Christmas in the City is a perfect village for collectors who want to enjoy all the splendor and sophistication of a booming metropolis from the comfort of their own homes. Like any great city, *Christmas in the City* is filled with magnificent cathedrals, world-renowned museums, trendy residential neighborhoods and the finest restaurants (including the new "Cafe Caprice French Restaurant"). First issued in 1987, the series has grown to include 38 individual lighted buildings, with 13 currently available.

North Pole©

    Fantasy comes to life with the whimsical *North Pole* series and with each new release, the fantasy world becomes more vivid and magical. The *North Pole* series began in 1991 with the debut of "Santa's Workshop" and the two-piece set of "Elf Bunkhouse" and "Reindeer Barn" (which features stalls with nameplates for Prancer, Vixen, Comet and Cupid). Since then the collection has grown to include 30 lighted buildings, with 19 currently available. Along the way, collectors have enjoyed glimpses of everyday life at the North Pole; the workshops where dedicated elves make dolls, bears and toy soldiers; the shops where candy and toys are tested to see what's most popular; and even several of Santa's little secrets like "Santa's Lookout Tower" (1993) where Santa can watch over the children of the world and the "Weather and Time Observatory" (1995) where he carefully maps out his Christmas Eve route. Among this year's releases is the cozy home Santa shares with his loving wife, "Route 1, North Pole, Home Of Mr. & Mrs. Claus." Several of the early releases in this series have retired in the past few years, including "Santa's Workshop" in 1993 which, according to secondary market demand, is one of the "coolest" pieces to have in your collection.

COLLECTOR'S
VALUE GUIDE™

Heritage Village Overview

Disney Parks Village Series©

Perhaps the most unique series in The Heritage Village Collection, this short-lived collection (introduced in 1994, retired in 1996) united the magic of Disney with the phenomenon of Department 56. The pieces in this collection were based on actual buildings in the Disney parks in Florida and California, which are among the world's most popular tourist attractions. Released in late 1994 at the Walt Disney theme parks and later at selected retailers, the series consisted of six lighted buildings and four accessories and captured the whimsical architecture of the parks' buildings.

The biggest news for the *Disney Parks Village Series* was the unexpected retirement of all six buildings and four accessories in May, 1996. The last two releases, "Silversmith" and "Tinker Bell's Treasures" have become a valuable find as they were available for only a short time before the series' sudden retirement.

Little Town of Bethlehem©

This inspiring nativity scene was introduced in its entirety in 1987 as a 12-piece set. It is a unique representation of the humble birthplace of Christ, with three lighted buildings and nine accessories. This collection is sold as a set and is still current.

What's New In Heritage Village

This section highlights the new Heritage Village releases for 1997.

DICKENS' VILLAGE ®

Gad's Hill Place . . . The sixth and final release in the *Charles Dickens' Signature Series*, "Gad's Hill Place" is home to Charles Dickens himself, and it's a popular gathering place for all who come to hear him read his famous tale, *A Christmas Carol*. A gold monogrammed flag boasting the initials "CD" hangs from the second story of the home. Built of red

brick and accented with gray, this historic hearth looks lovely decorated with wreaths for the Christmas holiday. The evergreen bushes at the base of the house are a nice complement, giving the home a friendly, lived-in feel. The roof is made of a dark gray brick and has three windows built into the attic. Picture windows dressed with light blue curtains adorn the front,

Gad's Hill Place - #57535
Dickens' Village

while the side features a covered, wooden porch painted blue and white. Limited to 1997 production, "Gad's Hill Place" is a fitting crowning release to the *Charles Dickens' Signature Series*.

The Melancholy Tavern . . . This old English pub is always a favorite among the locals of *Dickens' Village*. Held together by timber beams,

the tavern's weathered shutters and crooked sign set a familiar and comfortable atmosphere in which all patrons can shed their sorrows. Its patched roof and cracked exterior creates a sort of droopy character for this saloon, but the tavern's fine beverages and legendary soups and stews have lifted many

The Melancholy Tavern - #58347
Dickens' Village

a spirit through the years.

What's New In Heritage Village

Mulberrie Court . . . As *Dickens' Village* grows, so does the need for more and more residential structures. A black iron and brass fence secures the privacy of this exclusive dwelling. Decorated for the holidays in wreaths and bows, it establishes the building as one of prominence. The building is comprised of three towers constructed of solid, gray brick. Darker gray wood accents surround the windows, which are individually decorated with yellow, red and blue curtains. This stately uptown residence boasts character and prestige and will add instant elegance to your *Dickens' Village* display.

Mulberrie Court - #58345
Dickens' Village

Nettie Quinn Puppets & Marionettes . . . There's always a crowd gathered around Nettie Quinn's gold-trimmed puppet show window and collectors will be happy to see that they are just in time for the matinee! The Victorian-style shop is home to many marionettes handcrafted with the finest of care by the shop's own proprietor. Golden jesters hang from either side of the front window, fine complements to the hourly puppet shows that entertain passersby. The roof is graced with equine weathervanes, while the stucco face of the building bears charming, ornate decor that makes Nettie Quinn's establishment elegant as well as fun. With its crimson roof and bright green trim, "Nettie Quinn Puppets & Marionettes" is one of the most colorful new releases in *Dickens' Village*.

Nettie Quinn Puppets &
Marionettes - #58344
Dickens' Village

The Olde Camden Town Church . . . This English Tudor church stands proudly in the center of town, a beautiful monument for all villagers to see. An old-fashioned clock with Roman numerals on its face chimes on the hour and just before mass to let patrons know it's time for prayer. Large doors embrace the center of the church above which a lantern always burns. Ivy is strung along the arch of the doorway, providing

COLLECTOR'S
VALUE GUIDE™

What's New In Heritage Village

The Olde Camden Town
Church - #58346
Dickens' Village

a festive holiday frame for the red wooden doors while ivy crosses lay upon the stoned-faced building on either side of the entrance. To the right of "The Olde Camden Town Church" is an adjoining rectory with a private entrance enclosed by a picket fence. There is always light emanating from its window and the fence's unlocked swinging gate welcomes any who wish to enter!

Quilly's Antiques . . . You'll be sure to find antiques of exquisite value among the selection at this elegant boutique. Built in an English

Quilly's Antiques - #58348
Dickens' Village

Victorian style, the building itself appears proudly aged with its slanted rooftop and dual chimneys that have weathered over time. A large paneled window adorns the front wall, making window shopping easy for all passers-by while a grandfather clock outside the door serves as a reminder of the value of time. As patrons walk the creaky wood floors and sift through the treasures within, their senses will sing with nostalgia as they discover old rocking chairs, iron tea kettles and copper vases straight out of Grandmother's attic.

Dickens' Village Accessories . . . The Christmas season is well on its way in *Dickens' Village* and the streets are alive with the bustle of holiday shoppers. Packed with presents, "The Fezziwig Delivery Wagon" rushes through the streets on its special delivery mission. Pulled by a magnificent grey mare, this cart is ready for its journey, complete with

The Fezziwig Delivery
Wagon - #58400
Dickens' Village

Gingerbread Vendor
(set/2) - #58402
Dickens' Village

hanging lanterns to illuminate the way. Meanwhile in the center of town, the "Gingerbread Vendor" (set/2) brings a sledful of traditional confections to a small boy and girl who readily partake of the treats.

COLLECTOR'S
VALUE GUIDE™

What's New In Heritage Village

Bundled in their holiday finest, a couple takes a romantic spin around the square in the "Red Christmas Sulky" on their way to visit friends, complete with a gift basket of freshly-baked muffins.   In another corner of town, people gather around a stone platform to hear "*A Christmas Carol* Reading by Charles Dickens" (set/4). This piece is also available as a limited edition (LE-42,500) set of seven and is the first accessory to be introduced to the *Charles Dickens' Signature Series.*

The new year also brings two new pieces to the "Twelve Days of Dickens' Village" series which debuted in 1995. In "Seven Swans-A-Swimming" a couple enjoys the wintry air and the antics of seven swans while in "Eight Maids-A-Milking" the villagers are hard at work, pails in hand, cow nearby, getting milk for holiday meals.

Red Christmas Sulky
- #58401
Dickens' Village

| *A Christmas Carol* Reading By Charles Dickens (set/4) - #58403 *Dickens' Village* | *A Christmas Carol* Reading By Charles Dickens (set/7) - #58404 *Dickens' Village* | Seven Swans-A-Swimming - #58383 *Dickens' Village* | Eight Maids-A-Milking - #58384 *Dickens' Village* |

NEW ENGLAND VILLAGE ®

Bobwhite Cottage . . . This Victorian-style cottage provides a romantic wintry getaway for New England couples. Finely-constructed lattice-work and gold spires add detail to the simple design typical of *New England Village.* Wreaths adorning the second floor windows offer holiday cheer, while streams of light emerging from downstairs windows create dancing shadows on the evening's fresh fallen snow. On a clear night, residents of the cottage can cuddle on the front or side porch and gaze dreamily at the stars. Later, they can warm themselves by the fireplace with a hot cup of cocoa.

Bobwhite Cottage - #56576
New England Village

COLLECTOR'S
VALUE GUIDE™

What's New In Heritage Village

J. Hudson Stoveworks ... It's going to be a cold winter in New England and business is booming for this *New England Village* shop. In anticipation of the upcoming season, this business' proprietors have stocked up with plenty of modern and antique stoves. For villagers looking to purchase a new stove or to repair an old one, "J. Hudson Stoveworks" is the place to go for all of their heating needs.

J. Hudson Stoveworks - #56574
New England Village

Navigational Charts & Maps ... For anyone planning to sail the seven seas, venture around the world or just learn the lore of the countryside, this shop is the first step of the journey. The simplicity of this two-story building gives no hint of the minute details buried in the hundreds of maps inside – ironically, it would not be difficult for one to get lost amongst the abundant sets of directions. A weathervane adorns the top of the building, forecasting the winter winds while at any given time, travelers can be found sitting around the fireplace inside sharing tales of travel near and far.

Navigational Charts &
Maps - #56575
New England Village

New England Village Accessories ... Just keeping warm during the frigid winter months is a full-time job for some *New England Village* residents. Luckily, several local shops and vendors are working diligently to satisfy the community's craving for warmth.

Whenever the first cold spell hits New England, the "J. Hudson Stoveworks" becomes busier than ever! Two men load an already full wagon with brand new stoves from the shop in the new accessory, "A New Potbellied Stove For Christmas." The driver and mare patiently await their cargo as they prepare to set off on their delivery mission, bringing warmth to chilly New England households. And then it's back to the shop to stock up for another trip . . . and then another and another.

A New Potbellied Stove For
Christmas - #56593
New England Village

What's New In Heritage Village

There's nothing better on a cold winter night than settling down with a wool blanket. "Christmas Bazaar . . . Handmade Quilts" (set/2) displays a variety of comforters for any taste, offering great gift ideas for loved ones (and maybe even for oneself!). In front of the display, a mother holds up one up one of her handmade blankets to show off its fine craftsmanship, while her daughter practices her own skills with the crochet needle.

Christmas Bazaar . . .
Handmade Quilts
(set/2) - #56594
New England Village

And since it's not always practical to carry around a stove or quilt to keep warm, villagers should also make "Christmas Bazaar . . . Woolens & Preserves" (set/2) a stop on their holiday shopping agenda. Here a matronly woman sells handmade gloves and scarves just like Grandma used to make. Her little assistant is a walking advertisement for the bazaar, all bundled up in its goods. All of the shop's customers should be sure to pick up a jar of jelly and a hot apple pie because nothing warms the heart like a full stomach.

Christmas Bazaar . . .
Woolens & Preserves
(set/2) - #56595
New England Village

ALPINE VILLAGE ©

Danube Music Publisher . . . The sweet sound of music swirling around eminent purple towers beckon weary travelers to come in from the storm for a song or two. Messages printed in German, including the sign above the door, "Donau Musik Verlag," serve as an open invitation to enter the world of music which knows no international boundaries. Here the patrons don't mind if you can't carry a tune, especially if you're willing to play a few notes on the house glockenspiel. Typical of *Alpine Village*, this building offers vibrant blues, reds and purples as well as a finely-detailed exterior adorned with flowerpots abounding with seasonal flowers wrapped in ribbons and bows. For all the villagers' musical needs, "Danube Music Publisher" is the place to go – it's where the best alpenhorn players get their sheet music!

Danube Music Publisher
- #56173
Alpine Village

COLLECTOR'S
VALUE GUIDE™

What's New In Heritage Village

Alpine Village Accessories . . . The nutcracker is a favorite holiday gift idea and one can always count on finding the "Nutcracker Vendor & Cart" in the heart of the village square. Those interested in this seller's wares better get cracking soon, as his supply looks low and he's sure to sell out.

Nutcracker Vendor & Cart
- #56183
Alpine Village

CHRISTMAS IN THE CITY ®

Cafe Caprice French Restaurant . . . Holiday shopping can really work up an appetite and after a long day at the shops, the city dwellers settle down at "Cafe Caprice French Restaurant" for three floors of fine French cuisine. The brownstone front, the blue, white and red awnings and the French-style windows offer a glimpse of France while the aroma of sizzling flambé and freshly-baked croissants saturate the air for blocks, tempting the passers-by. The latest exotic restaurant to open its doors, "Cafe Caprice French Restaurant" is a fine addition to the eclectic *Christmas in the City* dining experience.

Cafe Caprice French
Restaurant - #58882
Christmas in the City

Grand Central Railway Station . . . As one of the first centers of travel, Grand Central Station is immortalized in this *Christmas in the City* piece. While the bay windows are brightened with large holiday wreaths, the balcony has been festively decorated with snow-covered Christmas trees.

Grand Central Railway
Station - #58881
Christmas in the City

Lanterns illuminate the way for travelers, guiding them to the train platforms, while a large, old-fashioned clock insures that commuters will make their trains on time. Doors on either side of the front of the building offer easy access to the platforms and the double doors to the lobby invite friends and family inside to await the arrival of loved ones. As the first train station in the series, "Grand Central Railway Station" is a must for your *Christmas in the City* downtown center.

What's New In Heritage Village

Christmas in the City Accessories . . . It's Christmastime in the city and everyone has something to do and somewhere to be. In "Going Home For The Holidays" (set/3), a family hurries for their train, arms full of suitcases and presents. It's the last call for the 6 p.m. express as the conductor checks his pocket watch and helps a family with their luggage. Another family rushes home with a sled in tow, carrying "The Family Tree," while others prefer the comfort and convenience of the "City Taxi" to cart their tree and presents home.

Going Home For The Holidays
(set/3) - #58896
Christmas in the City

The Family Tree
- #58895
Christmas in the City

City Taxi
- #58894
Christmas in the City

NORTH POLE ©

Christmas Bread Bakers . . . If nothing says loving like something in the oven, then this new bakery is bursting with love! The bakery bustles with activity as Santa's elves scurry around getting ready for the holiday season. And if that's not enough to keep them busy, signs posted on the building promise world-wide delivery and a variety of culinary delights from panettone to brioche. The actual structure of the building resembles loaves of bread and is decorated for the holidays with holly and strands of wheat.

Christmas Bread Bakers - #56393
North Pole

What's New In Heritage Village

Hall Of Records . . . All the well-known facts (and-not-so-well-known facts) of the North Pole lie within the four walls of this building. Snow decorates the rooftops and festive holly hangs about the walls offering holiday cheer. The tower's clock marks the time as the diligent "Hall Of Records" employees keep track of the past, present and future events of the North Pole. It's especially busy this time of year as the elves check their records once and then twice to find out who's been naughty and nice (the scroll above the door serves as a constant reminder to villagers of this task). Anyone wishing to go on a historical journey of the North Pole can venture into the stacks of the hall, but they're going to

Hall Of Records - #56392
North Pole

have to wait outside for a few minutes as the sign on the door states, "Out For Hot Chocolate, Back at 4:00."

Route 1, North Pole, Home Of Mr. & Mrs. Claus . . . This cozy gingerbread style house is a welcome sight for Santa's tired eyes the morning after Christmas Eve. But for poor Mr. Claus, the work is never done and there's only a few minutes rest until it's back to work making toys for the next year. The building is an appropriately majestic home for Father Christmas, with its bright red roof, festive green trim and many tall spires topped with gold "NP" flags. A big red mailbox stands at the entrance and needs to be emptied every few hours as millions of letters pour in year-round from all over the world. Cut-out Christmas trees adorn many swinging gates, providing easy access to the house for the constant traffic of elves and visitors alike. And there is never a quiet moment in this neighborhood, as the sounds of hammering and elves scurrying around can always be heard coming from the workshop entrance on the side of the building.

Route 1, North Pole, Home Of
Mr. & Mrs. Claus - #56391
North Pole

COLLECTOR'S
VALUE GUIDE™

What's New In Heritage Village

North Pole Accessories . . . It's almost Christmas and there's no time to rest as these diligent elves are up at the crack of dawn in "Early Rising Elves" (set/5). Dressed in the traditional apparel of their country, international elves prepare native treats for millions of hungry boys and girls around the world.

Early Rising Elves
(set/5) - #56369
North Pole

There's a lot of work to be done and the elves have enlisted the help of friends around the world to make some toys and ship them to the North Pole via "The North Pole Express." Overflowing with gifts, trees and furry friends, this train is on a non-stop journey to drop off its treasures at Santa's workshop, where it will turn around and make the journey many more times before the ever-anticipated Christmas Eve. Meanwhile, toys that don't have as far to go are rushed to the "pole" on the back of a bicycle in "Holiday Deliveries."

The North Pole Express
- #56368
North Pole

Holiday Deliveries
- #56371
North Pole

And now that it's all said and done and Santa has reached the "End Of The Line" (set/2), it looks as if he may have given himself a present – vacation time. With a camera around his neck, a box of fresh fruit at his companion's feet and a tell-tale Miami sticker on his suitcase (not to mention his sunglasses and Hawaiian shirt), Santa looks well rested and looks ready to go for next Christmas.

End Of The Line (set/2)
- #56370
North Pole

COLLECTOR'S
VALUE GUIDE™

What's New In Heritage Village

GENERAL HERITAGE VILLAGE ACCESSORIES

General Village Accessories . . . Heritage Village introduces three new animated accessories to give life to any of the Department 56 villages. The "Village Animated Ski Mountain," complete with lift, snowboarder and skier, brings wintry fun to any landscape. The "Village Waterfall" offers a chilly treat for those ready to brave the icy waters for a mid-winter swim or for those who just wish to relax by the sounds of rushing water. The "Village Animated Accessory Track" is the perfect way to "motorize" your display. The track is large enough for you to put several pieces in the center and many new accessories are specifically designed to complement the track. Seeing villagers strolling around the buildings is an impressive sight!

Village Animated Ski
Mountain - #52641
Heritage Village

Village Waterfall
- #52644
Heritage Village

Village Animated Accessory
Track - #52462
Heritage Village

What's New In Heritage Village

Recent Retirements

Department 56 announces new retirements for Heritage Village each year and for the past several years the list has been published in *USA Today*. The following pieces (listed with issue year in parentheses) were retired on November 8, 1996, except for the entire *Disney Parks Village Series*, which was retired in May.

Dickens' Village
- ❑ The Grapes Inn (1996)
- ❑ King's Road (1990, set/2)
    C.H. Watt Physician
    Tutbury Printer
- ❑ Kingsford's Brewhouse (1993)
- ❑ Old Michaelchurch (1992)
- ❑ Pump Lane Shoppes (1993, set/3)
    Bumpstead Nye Cloaks & Canes
    Lomas Ltd. Molasses
    W.M. Wheat Cakes & Puddings
- ❑ Ramsford Palace (1996, set/17)
- ❑ Start A Tradition Set (1995, set/13)
    Town Square Carolers (set/3)
    Town Square Shops (set/2)
    Faversham Lamps & Oil
    Morston Steak & Kidney Pie
- ❑ C. Bradford Wheelwright & Son
    (1993, set/2, *accessory*)
- ❑ Vision Of A Christmas Past
    (1993, set/3, *accessory*)

New England Village
- ❑ A. Bieler Farm (1993, set/2)
    Pennsylvania Dutch Barn
    Pennsylvania Dutch Farmhouse
- ❑ Bluebird Seed And Bulb (1992)
- ❑ Captain's Cottage (1990)
- ❑ Knife Grinder (1993, set/2, *accessory*)

Alpine Village
- ❑ Alpine Village (1986, set/5) Δ
    Besson Bierkeller
    Gasthof Eisl
    Milch-Kase

Δ only three pieces in this set of five are retired. The other two pieces, "Apotheke" and "E. Staubr Backer," are still currently available.

Christmas in the City
- ❑ Uptown Shoppes (1992, set/3)
    City Clockworks
    Haberdashery
    Music Emporium
- ❑ West Village Shops (1993, set/2)
    Potter's Tea Seller
    Spring St. Coffee House
- ❑ Automobiles (1987, set/3, *accessory*)

North Pole
- ❑ Elfie's Sleds & Skates (1992)
- ❑ North Pole (1990, set/2) ◊
    Elf Bunkhouse
- ❑ Obbie's Books & Letrinka's Candy (1992)
- ❑ Santa's Woodworks (1993)
- ❑ Start A Tradition Set (1996, set/12)
    Candy Cane & Peppermint Shop
    Gift Wrap & Ribbons

Disney Parks Village Series
This entire series of six lighted buildings and four accessories was retired in May, 1996.

General Heritage Village Accessories
- ❑ Christmas Bells (1996)
- ❑ Playing In The Snow (1993, set/3)
- ❑ Village Express Train (1988, set/22)
- ❑ Village Express Van (1992)

◊ the other piece in this set of two, "Reindeer Barn," is still currently available.

Heritage Village Top Ten

    This section highlights the ten most valuable retired Heritage Village pieces as determined by their secondary market value. To qualify for the top ten, pieces have to have top dollar value and show a significant percentage increase in value from their original prices (as shown by our "market meter"). Many of the top ten pieces are limited editions, while others were produced for only two years or experienced production problems that decreased the number of available pieces. Five of the top ten are from Dickens' Village, two each from New England Village and Christmas in the City, and one from Alpine Village. An "honorable mention" goes to "Sutton Place Brownstones" from Christmas in the City.

#1   DICKENS' VILLAGE MILL (LE-2,500)

Dickens' Village, #6519-6
Issued 1985 — Retired 1986
Issue Price: $35
Secondary Market Price: $5,080
Market Meter: +14,414%

    The most valuable Heritage Village piece on the secondary market is the "Dickens' Village Mill," the very first limited edition building in the collection. The fact that there were only 2,500 pieces produced didn't cause much of a stir when the mill was issued in 1985. Early "collectors" may have just stumbled onto the mill in stores, not realizing that it was a limited edition. Only *after the fact* did people realize what they had missed, and by that time, there were a greater number of collectors looking for the same piece. In the ten years since its retirement in 1986, the secondary market value of the "Dickens' Village Mill" has increased by a startling 14,414%! With its limited availability and high demand, "The Mill" is considered by many to be the crown jewel of their collection – or the one that got away.

COLLECTOR'S
VALUE GUIDE™

#2 NORMAN CHURCH (LE-3,500)

Dickens' Village, #6502-1
Issued 1986 — Retired 1987
Issue Price: $40
Secondary Market Price: $3,225
Market Meter: +7,963%

"Norman Church" was the second limited edition in *Dickens' Village* and was limited to 3,500 pieces. To put the limited quantity of the "Norman Church" in perspective, the limited editions that were released the following two years more than doubled ("Chesterton Manor House," LE-7,500) and tripled ("C. Fletcher Public House," LE-12,500) in the number of pieces available. The large "Norman Church" fit very snugly in its original box, so collectors who were concerned about damaging the piece slit part of the box and the sleeve so the piece would fit better. Many boxes and sleeves that were cut this way wore out over time which has made it very difficult to find a "Norman Church" that comes with its original packaging.

#3 CATHEDRAL CHURCH OF ST. MARK (LE-3,024)

Christmas in the City, #5549-2
Issued 1991 — Retired 1993
Issue Price: $120
Secondary Market Price: $2,075
Market Meter: +1,629%

Originally scheduled for a limited edition run of 17,500, the grand "Cathedral Church Of St. Mark" from the *Christmas in the City* collection suffered serious production problems very early on. Thousands of pieces had to be destroyed and by the time production was halted, 3,024 had been shipped. Some pieces had production flaws such as firing cracks, and many of these were returned by retailers, which reduced the actual number of available pieces to *less than* 3,024. Collectors hadn't seen an edition size this small since the first two limited editions in *Dickens' Village* and the rush for pieces caused an incredible secondary market frenzy in 1993 and 1994, which has just recently started to slow down. The "Cathedral Church of St. Mark" is the only non-*Dickens' Village* piece among the top five most valuable Heritage Village pieces.

#4 CHESTERTON MANOR HOUSE (LE-7,500)

Dickens' Village, #6568-4
Issued 1987 — Retired 1988
Issue Price: $45
Secondary Market Price: $1,720
Market Meter: +3,722%

"Chesterton Manor House" was the third limited edition in *Dickens' Village* and its stately elegance has proven to be very popular with collectors to this day. However, collectors should be certain to check their "Chesterton Manor House" pieces carefully, as firing and stress cracks are not uncommon with this piece. Also, the chimneys were very fragile; if you purchased the piece on the secondary market, you might find the chimney had broken off and been reattached with glue. Any of these problems are likely to lower the secondary market value of the piece. The limited edition quantity of 7,500 pieces is small to begin with, but the slight problems with many pieces means that the actual number of manor houses available in mint condition is even smaller.

#5 THE ORIGINAL SHOPS OF DICKENS' VILLAGE (SET/7)

Dickens' Village, #6515-3
Issued 1984 — Retired 1988
Issue Price: $175
Secondary Market Price: $1,360
Market Meter: +677%

Although "The Original Shops Of Dickens' Village" (set/7) was available for four years, it has proven to be a valuable commodity on the secondary market. One reason is that few early collectors realized that the seven quaint shops would be the start of a collectible phenomenon. By the time the set was retired in 1988, more complex and colorful designs were available, which made the duller-colored shops less attractive to collectors. Retailers ordered fewer sets as a result, and this has contributed to the secondary market demand. In general, the more colorful buildings (such as "Crowntree Inn") are in higher demand than the shops with more muted color tones ("Abel Beesley Butcher"). Although the pieces were released as a set, some retailers sold them separately and it is not uncommon to still find individual pieces on the secondary market.

Crowntree Inn

Candle Shop

The Original Shops Of Dickens' Village

Green Grocer

Golden Swan Baker

Bean & Son Smithy Shop

Abel Beesley Butcher

Jones & Co.
Brush & Basket Shop

#6 NEW ENGLAND VILLAGE (SET/7)

New England Village, #6530-7
Issued 1986 — Retired 1989
Issue Price: $170
Secondary Market Price: $1,280
Market Meter: +653%

Right behind the "Original Shops Of Dickens' Village" (set/7) is another seven-piece debut set, "New England Village" (set/7). Like its *Dickens' Village* counterpart, this set was available for four years and offered the core pieces for a genuine New England township. An important point is that "Steeple Church" (item #6530-7), which was sold as part of the set, was also available individually as a separate piece with a new item number (#6539-0). Remember that the piece with the latter item number is not officially part of the seven-piece set.

Apothecary Shop

General Store

Nathaniel Bingham
Fabrics

New England Village

Livery Stable &
Boot Shop

Steeple Church

Brick Town Hall

Red Schoolhouse

COLLECTOR'S
VALUE GUIDE™

#7 SMYTHE WOOLEN MILL (LE-7,500)

New England Village, #6543-9
Issued 1987 — Retired 1988
Issue Price: $42
Secondary Market Price: $1,180
Market Meter: +2,710%

The second mill represented in the Top Ten is the "Smythe Woolen Mill," which has been the only limited edition piece in *New England Village* to date. Its relatively small production run (LE-7,500) made it highly coveted when it was first released in 1987. This fact becomes even more important when you consider the tremendous cross-over appeal of "Smythe Woolen Mill." *New England Village* collectors had to compete not only with each other to find the piece, but also with *Dickens' Village* enthusiasts, who remembered their experience with the highly limited "Dickens' Village Mill" three years before. This makes the "Smythe Woolen Mill" a challenging find on the secondary market.

#8 JOSEF ENGEL FARMHOUSE

Alpine Village, #5952-8
Issued 1987 — Retired 1989
Issue Price: $33
Secondary Market Price: $980
Market Meter: +2,870%

The only *Alpine Village* piece in the Top Ten, "Josef Engel Farmhouse" was the first piece to retire from the village and has steadily increased in value on the secondary market. It was in production for only two years and it attracted the attention of *New England Village* collectors, who did not have a farmhouse of their own until 1989. It may be very difficult to find a "Josef Engel Farmhouse" that is in mint condition, as the tiny, sharp corners in the design led to many small chips and nicks.

#9 DICKENS' COTTAGES (SET/3)

Dickens' Village, #6518-8
Issued 1985 — Retired 1988
Issue Price: $75
Secondary Market Price: $975
Market Meter: +1200%

These three cottages did not make a great impression with collectors when they were first issued in 1985. Although they were the first private homes in *Dickens' Village* and the set was available for four years, the drab color tones of the pieces failed to catch the eye of collectors, especially in comparison with brighter, more creative releases such as the "Christmas Carol Cottages" (set/3) and "David Copperfield" (set/3). Also, the names of the three "Dickens' Cottages" never appeared on the pieces at all, and did not appear on the sleeves until 1987. Because of all these factors, fewer sets were ordered by retailers and fewer sets reached collectors' hands – which means that the cottages are now highly sought after on the secondary market.

Thatched Cottage   Stone Cottage   Tudor Cottage

#10 PALACE THEATRE

Christmas in the City, #5963-3
Issued 1987 — Retired 1989
Issue Price: $45
Secondary Market Price: $960
Market Meter: +2,033%

Although the "Palace Theatre" is not the most valuable retired Heritage Village piece, it may have the most interesting history. This *Christmas in the City* piece was in production for only two years; production problems, such as concave walls, and breakage during shipping decreased the number of pieces sold by retailers. Most importantly, at the time "Palace Theatre" was retired, rumors swirled that a large shipment of pieces never reached retailers, creating an "instant shortage." These rumors caused a panic among collectors and drove the secondary market value sky high in a very short time (over $1,000 by 1992). Only recently has the value of the "Palace Theatre" descended to what many think are more realistic levels.

HONORABLE MENTION:

SUTTON PLACE BROWNSTONES

Christmas in the City, #5961-7
Issued 1987— Retired 1989
Issue Price: $80
Secondary Market Price: $900
Market Meter: +1,025%

The "Sutton Place Brownstones" were the very first apartment buildings released in *Christmas in the City*. As this piece was available for only two years, many collectors missed their chance to add it to their collections. While other apartment buildings have been released since the retirement of the "Sutton Place Brownstones," many collectors consider the status of owning the "original" brownstones worth the price.

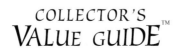

COLLECTOR'S
VALUE GUIDE™

How To Use Your Value Guide

This section lists the entire Heritage Village Collection and is split up by village in the following order: *Dickens' Village, New England Village, Alpine Village, Christmas in the City, North Pole, Disney Parks Village Series* and *Little Town of Bethlehem*. Lighted buildings are listed first, followed by a separate section of accessories. Every building and accessory is listed alphabetically, making it easy to find your pieces.

How To Total The Value Of Your Collection

The value guide is a great way to keep track of the value of your collection. Simply fill in the blanks for the pieces you own. Put down the year you purchased the piece and the price paid. From the "Market Value" column, find the value and record it in the "Value of My Collection" column.

*Write the **Market Value** of your pieces in the **Value of My Collection** column*

	DICKENS' VILLAGE	Original Price	Status	Market Value	Year Purch.	Price Paid	Value of My Collection
1.	Great Denton Mill	$50.00	Current	$50.00	1995	50	50
2.	Green Gate Cottage (LE-22,500)	$64.00	Retired	$295.00			
3.	Hather Harness	$48.00	Current	$48.00			
4.	Hembleton Pewterer	$72.00	Retired	$89.00	1993	72	89
5.	Ivy Glen Church	$35.00	Retired	$96.00	1990	35	96
6.	J.D. Nichols Toy Shop	$48.00	Current	$50.00			
7.	Kenilworth Castle	$70.00	Retired	$715.00	1988	70	715
8.	King's Road (set/2)	$72.00	Retired	$104.00	1992	72	104
a	*C.H. Watt Physician*	$36.00		$48.00			
b	*Tutbury Printer*	$36.00		$48.00			
			PENCIL TOTALS			299	1,054
						Price Paid	Market Value

You can then total the columns at the bottom of the page (use a pencil so you can change totals as your collection grows) and transfer each subtotal to the summary page at the end of the section to come up with the total value of your collection.

COLLECTOR'S
VALUE GUIDE™

	#5555-7	#5900-5	#5900-5
(1) 	(2a) 	(2b) 	
Ashbury Inn Issued: 1991 • Retired: 1995	**Barley Bree** *Barn* Issued: 1987 • Retired: 1989	**Barley Bree** *Farmhouse* Issued: 1987 • Retired: 1989	

	#5567-0	#58330	#6508-0
(3) 	(4)	(5) 	
Bishops Oast House Issued: 1990 • Retired: 1992	**Blenham Street Bank** Issued: 1995 • Current	**Blythe Pond Mill House** Issued: 1986 • Retired: 1990	

	#5809-2	#5810-6	#6549-8
(6) 	(7) 	(8)	
Boarding & Lodging School ("18") Issued: 1993 • Retired: 1993	**Boarding & Lodging School ("43")** Issued: 1994 • Current	**Brick Abbey** Issued: 1987 • Retired: 1989	

	DICKENS' VILLAGE	Original Price	Status	Market Value	Year Purch.	Price Paid	Value of My Collection
1.	Ashbury Inn	$55.00	Retired	$78.00			
2.	Barley Bree (set/2)	$60.00	Retired	$400.00			
a	*Barn*	$30.00		not established			
b	*Farmhouse*	$30.00		not established			
3.	Bishops Oast House	$45.00	Retired	$84.00			
4.	Blenham Street Bank	$60.00	Current	$60.00			
5.	Blythe Pond Mill House • Variation: By The Pond	$37.00	Retired	$305.00 $145.00			
6.	Boarding & Lodging School ("18")	$48.00	Retired	$186.00			
7.	Boarding & Lodging School ("43")	$48.00	Current	$48.00			
8.	Brick Abbey	$33.00	Retired	$396.00			

✎ **PENCIL TOTALS**

	PRICE PAID	MARKET VALUE

#58338

Butter Tub Barn
Issued: 1996 • Current

#58337

Butter Tub Farmhouse
Issued: 1996 • Current

#5904-8

C. Fletcher Public House
(LE-12,500)
Issued: 1988 • Retired: 1989

#6528-5

Chadbury Station And Train
Issued: 1986 • Retired: 1989

#6568-4

Chesterton Manor House
(LE-7,500)
Issued: 1987 • Retired: 1988

#58339

Christmas Carol Cottage,
Revisited
(w/smoking chimney)
Issued: 1996 • Current

#6500-5

Christmas Carol Cottages
The Cottage Of Bob Cratchit &
Tiny Tim
Issued: 1986 • Retired: 1995

#6500-5

Christmas Carol Cottages
Fezziwig's Warehouse
Issued: 1986 • Retired: 1995

#6500-5

Christmas Carol Cottages
Scrooge & Marley Counting
House
Issued: 1986 • Retired: 1995

	DICKENS' VILLAGE	Original Price	Status	Market Value	Year Purch.	Price Paid	Value of My Collection
1.	Butter Tub Barn	$48.00	Current	$48.00			
2.	Butter Tub Farmhouse	$40.00	Current	$40.00			
3.	C. Fletcher Public House (LE-12,500)	$35.00	Retired	$570.00			
4.	Chadbury Station And Train	$65.00	Retired	$400.00			
5.	Chesterton Manor House (LE-7,500)	$45.00	Retired	$1720.00			
6.	Christmas Carol Cottage, Revisited	$60.00	Current	$60.00			
7.	Christmas Carol Cottages (set/3)	$75.00	Retired	$135.00			
a	*The Cottage Of Bob Cratchit & Tiny Tim*	$25.00		$65.00			
b	*Fezziwig's Warehouse*	$25.00		$44.00			
c	*Scrooge & Marley Counting House*	$25.00		$55.00			

✎ **PENCIL TOTALS**

Price Paid	Market Value

DICKENS' VILLAGE

#5924-2

1a

Cobblestone Shops
Booter And Cobbler
Issued: 1988 • Retired: 1990

#5924-2

1b

Cobblestone Shops
T. Wells Fruit & Spice Shop
Issued: 1988 • Retired: 1990

#5924-2

1c

Cobblestone Shops
The Wool Shop
Issued: 1988 • Retired: 1990

#5583-2

2

Cobles Police Station
Issued: 1989 • Retired: 1991

#5902-1

3

**Counting House & Silas
Thimbleton Barrister**
Issued: 1988 • Retired: 1990

#5750-9

4

Crown & Cricket Inn
Issued: 1992 • Retired: 1992
Charles Dickens' Signature Series

#5550-6

5a

David Copperfield
Betsy Trotwood's Cottage
Issued: 1989 • Retired: 1992

#5550-6

5b

David Copperfield
Mr. Wickfield Solicitor
Issued: 1989 • Retired: 1992

#5550-6

5c

David Copperfield
Peggotty's Seaside Cottage
Issued: 1989 • Retired: 1992

	DICKENS' VILLAGE	Original Price	Status	Market Value	Year Purch.	Price Paid	Value of My Collection
1.	Cobblestone Shops (set/3)	$95.00	Retired	$393.00			
a	*Booter And Cobbler*	$32.00		$132.00			
b	*T. Wells Fruit & Spice Shop*	$32.00		$99.00			
c	*The Wool Shop*	$32.00		$195.00			
2.	Cobles Police Station	$37.50	Retired	$150.00			
3.	Counting House & Silas Thimbleton Barrister	$32.00	Retired	$96.00			
4.	Crown & Cricket Inn (Charles Dickens' Signature Series)	$100.00	Retired	$177.00			
5.	David Copperfield (set/3) • Variation: Set w/tan Peggotty's	$125.00	Retired	$184.00 $265.00			
a	*Betsy Trotwood's Cottage*	$42.50		$68.00			
b	*Mr. Wickfield Solicitor*	$42.50		$92.00			
c	*Peggotty's Seaside Cottage* • Variation: tan	$42.50		$70.00 $148.00			

✎ **PENCIL TOTALS**

PRICE PAID	MARKET VALUE

DICKENS' VILLAGE

#5752-5

Dedlock Arms
Issued: 1994 • Retired: 1994
Charles Dickens' Signature Series

#6518-8

Dickens' Cottages
Stone Cottage
Issued: 1985 • Retired: 1988

#6518-8

Dickens' Cottages
Thatched Cottage
Issued: 1985 • Retired: 1988

#6518-8

Dickens' Cottages
Tudor Cottage
Issued: 1985 • Retired: 1988

#6507-2

Dickens' Lane Shops
Cottage Toy Shop
Issued: 1986 • Retired: 1989

#6507-2

Dickens' Lane Shops
Thomas Kersey Coffee House
Issued: 1986 • Retired: 1989

#6507-2

Dickens' Lane Shops
Tuttle's Pub
Issued: 1986 • Retired: 1989

DICKENS' VILLAGE	Original Price	Status	Market Value	Year Purch.	Price Paid	Value of My Collection
1. Dedlock Arms (Charles Dickens' Signature Series)	$100.00	Retired	$154.00			
2. Dickens' Cottages (set/3)	$75.00	Retired	$975.00			
• Variation: Set w/tan Stone Cottage			$1050.00			
a Stone Cottage	$25.00		$425.00			
• Variation: tan			$520.00			
b Thatched Cottage	$25.00		$198.00			
c Tudor Cottage	$25.00		$415.00			
3. Dickens' Lane Shops (set/3)	$80.00	Retired	$642.00			
a Cottage Toy Shop	$27.00		$245.00			
b Thomas Kersey Coffee House	$27.00		$185.00			
c Tuttle's Pub	$27.00		$240.00			

✎ **PENCIL TOTALS**

PRICE PAID	MARKET VALUE

(1) #6516-1

Dickens' Village Church
Issued: 1985 • Retired: 1989

(2) #6519-6

Dickens' Village Mill (LE-2,500)
Issued: 1985 • Retired: 1986

(3) #5834-3

Dudden Cross Church
Issued: 1995 • Current

(4) #58329

Dursley Manor
Issued: 1995 • Current

(5) #5552-2

Fagin's Hide-A-Way
Issued: 1991 • Retired: 1995

(6) #5587-5

The Flat Of Ebenezer Scrooge
Issued: 1989 • Current

(7) #57535 NEW!

Gad's Hill Place
Issued: 1997 • Current
Charles Dickens' Signature Series

(8) #5822-0

Giggelswick Mutton & Ham
Issued: 1994 • Current

(9) #57534

The Grapes Inn
Issued: 1996 • Retired: 1996
Charles Dickens' Signature Series

	DICKENS' VILLAGE	Original Price	Status	Market Value	Year Purch.	Price Paid	Value of My Collection
1.	Dickens' Village Church	$35.00	Retired	---			
	• Variation: Dark/Butterscotch			$182.00			
	• Variation: Green			$343.00			
	• Variation: Tan			$195.00			
	• Variation: White			$415.00			
	• Variation: Yellow/Cream			$290.00			
2.	Dickens' Village Mill (LE-2,500)	$35.00	Retired	$5080.00			
3.	Dudden Cross Church	$45.00	Current	$45.00			
4.	Dursley Manor	$50.00	Current	$55.00			
5.	Fagin's Hide-A-Way	$68.00	Retired	$96.00			
6.	The Flat Of Ebenezer Scrooge	$37.50	Current	$37.50			
7.	Gad's Hill Place (Charles Dickens' Signature Series)	$98.00	Current	$98.00			
8.	Giggelswick Mutton & Ham	$48.00	Current	$48.00			
9.	The Grapes Inn (Charles Dickens' Signature Series)	$120.00	Retired	$145.00			

✎ **PENCIL TOTALS**

	PRICE PAID	MARKET VALUE

1	#5812-2
2	#5586-7
3	#5823-8

Great Denton Mill
Issued: 1993 • Current

Green Gate Cottage (LE-22,500)
Issued: 1989 • Retired: 1990

Hather Harness
Issued: 1994 • Current

4	#5800-9
5	#5927-7
6	#58328

Hembleton Pewterer
Issued: 1992 • Retired: 1995

Ivy Glen Church
Issued: 1988 • Retired: 1991

J.D. Nichols Toy Shop
Issued: 1995 • Current

7	#5916-1
8a	#5568-9
8b	#5568-9

Kenilworth Castle
Issued: 1987 • Retired: 1988

King's Road
C.H. Watt Physician (#55691)
Issued: 1990 • Retired: 1996

King's Road
Tutbury Printer (#55690)
Issued: 1990 • Retired: 1996

	Dickens' Village	Original Price	Status	Market Value	Year Purch.	Price Paid	Value of My Collection
1.	Great Denton Mill	$50.00	Current	$50.00			
2.	Green Gate Cottage (LE-22,500)	$64.00	Retired	$295.00			
3.	Hather Harness	$48.00	Current	$48.00			
4.	Hembleton Pewterer	$72.00	Retired	$89.00			
5.	Ivy Glen Church	$35.00	Retired	$96.00			
6.	J.D. Nichols Toy Shop	$48.00	Current	$50.00			
7.	Kenilworth Castle	$70.00	Retired	$715.00			
8.	King's Road (set/2)	$72.00	Retired	$104.00			
a	*C.H. Watt Physician*	$36.00		$48.00			
b	*Tutbury Printer*	$36.00		$48.00			
				PENCIL TOTALS			
						Price Paid	Market Value

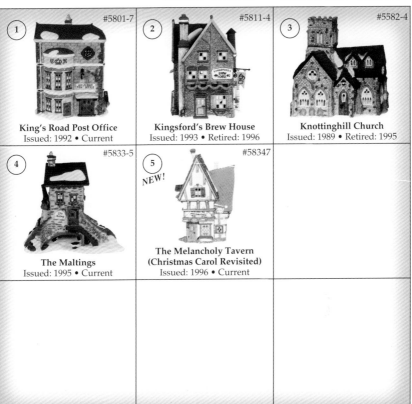

DICKENS' VILLAGE

#5801-7
1
King's Road Post Office
Issued: 1992 • Current

#5811-4
2
Kingsford's Brew House
Issued: 1993 • Retired: 1996

#5582-4
3
Knottinghill Church
Issued: 1989 • Retired: 1995

#5833-5
4
The Maltings
Issued: 1995 • Current

#58347
5
NEW!
The Melancholy Tavern
(Christmas Carol Revisited)
Issued: 1996 • Current

DICKENS' VILLAGE	Original Price	Status	Market Value	Year Purch.	Price Paid	Value of My Collection
1. King's Road Post Office	$45.00	Current	$45.00			
2. Kingsford's Brew House	$45.00	Retired	$63.00			
3. Knottinghill Church	$50.00	Retired	$75.00			
4. The Maltings	$50.00	Current	$50.00			
5. The Melancholy Tavern (Christmas Carol Revisited)	$45.00	Current	$45.00			
PENCIL TOTALS					Price Paid	Market Value

1a #5926-9
Merchant Shops
Geo. Weeton Watchmaker
Issued: 1988 • Retired: 1993

1b #5926-9
Merchant Shops
The Mermaid Fish Shoppe
Issued: 1988 • Retired: 1993

1c #5926-9
Merchant Shops
Poulterer
Issued: 1988 • Retired: 1993

1d #5926-9
Merchant Shops
Walpole Tailors
Issued: 1988 • Retired: 1993

1e #5926-9
Merchant Shops
White Horse Bakery
Issued: 1988 • Retired: 1993

2 NEW! #58345
Mulberrie Court
Issued: 1996 • Current

3 #5557-3
Nephew Fred's Flat
Issued: 1991 • Retired: 1994

4 NEW! #58344
Nettie Quinn Puppets &
Marionettes
Issued: 1996 • Current

	DICKENS' VILLAGE	Original Price	Status	Market Value	Year Purch.	Price Paid	Value of My Collection
1.	Merchant Shops (set/5)	$150.00	Retired	$260.00			
a	*Geo. Weeton Watchmaker*	$32.50		$63.00			
b	*The Mermaid Fish Shoppe*	$32.50		$77.00			
c	*Poulterer*	$32.50		$64.00			
d	*Walpole Tailors*	$32.50		$63.00			
e	*White Horse Bakery*	$32.50		$65.00			
2.	Mulberrie Court	$90.00	Current	$90.00			
3.	Nephew Fred's Flat	$35.00	Retired	$80.00			
4.	Nettie Quinn Puppets & Marionettes	$50.00	Current	$50.00			

✏ PENCIL TOTALS

PRICE PAID	MARKET VALUE

#5925-0 (1a)

Nicholas Nickleby
Nicholas Nickleby Cottage
Issued: 1988 • Retired: 1991

#5925-0 (1b)

Nicholas Nickleby
Wackford Squeers Boarding School
Issued: 1988 • Retired: 1991

#6502-1 (2)

Norman Church (LE-3,500)
Issued: 1986 • Retired: 1987

#5905-6 (3)

The Old Curiosity Shop
Issued: 1987 • Current

#5562-0 (4)

Old Michaelchurch
Issued: 1992 • Retired: 1996

#58346 (5) NEW!

**The Olde Camden Town Church
(Christmas Carol Revisited)**
Issued: 1996 • Current

#5553-0 (6a)

Oliver Twist
Brownlow House
Issued: 1991 • Retired: 1993

#5553-0 (6b)

Oliver Twist
Maylie Cottage
Issued: 1991 • Retired: 1993

DICKENS' VILLAGE	Original Price	Status	Market Value	Year Purch.	Price Paid	Value of My Collection
1. Nicholas Nickleby (set/2)	$72.00	Retired	$175.00			
• Variation: Set w/misspelled cottage			$209.00			
a Nicholas Nickleby Cottage	$36.00		$95.00			
• Variation: Nic"k"olas misspelled			$132.00			
b Wackford Squeers Boarding School	$36.00		$96.00			
2. Norman Church (LE-3,500)	$40.00	Retired	$3225.00			
3. The Old Curiosity Shop	$30.00	Current	$45.00			
4. Old Michaelchurch	$42.00	Retired	$62.00			
5. The Olde Camden Town Church (Christmas Carol Revisited)	$55.00	Current	$55.00			
6. Oliver Twist (set/2)	$75.00	Retired	$145.00			
a Brownlow House	$37.50		$80.00			
b Maylie Cottage	$37.50		$70.00			

✎ **PENCIL TOTALS**

PRICE PAID	MARKET VALUE

(1a) #6515-3

The Original Shops Of
Dickens' Village
Abel Beesley Butcher
Issued: 1984 • Retired: 1988

(1b) #6515-3

The Original Shops Of
Dickens' Village
Bean And Son Smithy Shop
Issued: 1984 • Retired: 1988

(1c) #6515-3

The Original Shops Of
Dickens' Village
Candle Shop
Issued: 1984 • Retired: 1988

(1d) #6515-3

The Original Shops Of
Dickens' Village
Crowntree Inn
Issued: 1984 • Retired: 1988

(1e) #6515-3

The Original Shops Of
Dickens' Village
Golden Swan Baker
Issued: 1984 • Retired: 1988

(1f) #6515-3

The Original Shops Of
Dickens' Village
Green Grocer
Issued: 1984 • Retired: 1988

(1g) #6515-3

The Original Shops Of
Dickens' Village
Jones & Co. Brush & Basket Shop
Issued: 1984 • Retired: 1988

(2) #5751-7

The Pied Bull Inn
Issued: 1993 • Retired: 1993
Charles Dickens' Signature Series

	DICKENS' VILLAGE	Original Price	Status	Market Value	Year Purch.	Price Paid	Value of My Collection
1.	The Original Shops of Dickens' Village (set/7)	$175.00	Retired	$1360.00			
a	*Abel Beesley Butcher*	$25.00		$136.00			
b	*Bean And Son Smithy Shop*	$25.00		$203.00			
c	*Candle Shop*	$25.00		$207.00			
d	*Crowntree Inn*	$25.00		$324.00			
e	*Golden Swan Baker*	$25.00		$190.00			
f	*Green Grocer*	$25.00		$208.00			
g	*Jones & Co. Brush & Basket Shop*	$25.00		$315.00			
2.	The Pied Bull Inn (Charles Dickens' Signature Series)	$100.00	Retired	$163.00			

🖉 **PENCIL TOTALS**

PRICE PAID	MARKET VALUE

DICKENS' VILLAGE

#5824-6

(1a)

Portobello Road Thatched
Cottages
Browning Cottage
Issued: 1994 • Current

#5824-6

(1b)

Portobello Road Thatched
Cottages
Cobb Cottage
Issued: 1994 • Current

#5824-6

(1c)

Portobello Road Thatched
Cottages
Mr. & Mrs. Pickle
Issued: 1994 • Current

#5808-4

(2a)

Pump Lane Shoppes
Bumpstead Nye Cloaks & Canes
(#58085)
Issued: 1993 • Retired: 1996

#5808-4

(2b)

Pump Lane Shoppes
Lomas Ltd. Molasses
(#58086)
Issued: 1993 • Retired: 1996

#5808-4

(2c)

Pump Lane Shoppes
W.M. Wheat Cakes & Puddings
(#58087)
Issued: 1993 • Retired: 1996

#58348

(3)

NEW!

Quilly's Antiques
Issued: 1996 • Current

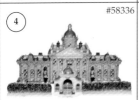

#58336

(4)

Ramsford Palace
(set/17, LE-27,500)
Issued: 1996 • Retired: 1996

#5585-9

(5)

Ruth Marion Scotch Woolens
(LE-17,500)
Issued: 1989 • Retired: 1990

DICKENS' VILLAGE	Original Price	Status	Market Value	Year Purch.	Price Paid	Value of My Collection
1. Portobello Road Thatched Cottages (set/3)	$120.00	Current	$120.00			
a *Browning Cottage*	$40.00		$40.00			
b *Cobb Cottage*	$40.00		$40.00			
c *Mr. & Mrs. Pickle*	$40.00		$40.00			
2. Pump Lane Shoppes (set/3)	$112.00	Retired	$142.00			
a *Bumpstead Nye Cloaks & Canes*	$37.50		$48.00			
b *Lomas Ltd. Molasses*	$37.50		$48.00			
c *W.M. Wheat Cakes & Puddings*	$37.50		$48.00			
3. Quilly's Antiques	$46.00	Current	$46.00			
4. Ramsford Palace (set/17, LE-27,500)	$175.00	Retired	$650.00			
5. Ruth Marion Scotch Woolens (LE-17,500)	$65.00	Retired	$400.00			

✎ **PENCIL TOTALS**

	PRICE PAID	MARKET VALUE

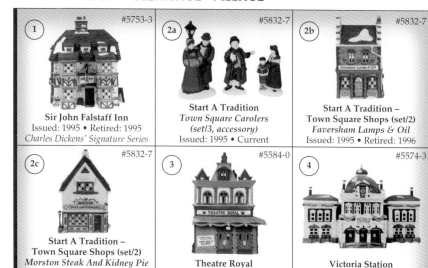

(1) #5753-3

Sir John Falstaff Inn
Issued: 1995 • Retired: 1995
Charles Dickens' Signature Series

(2a) #5832-7

Start A Tradition
Town Square Carolers
(set/3, accessory)
Issued: 1995 • Current

(2b) #5832-7

Start A Tradition –
Town Square Shops (set/2)
Faversham Lamps & Oil
Issued: 1995 • Retired: 1996

(2c) #5832-7

Start A Tradition –
Town Square Shops (set/2)
Morston Steak And Kidney Pie
Issued: 1995 • Current

(3) #5584-0

Theatre Royal
Issued: 1989 • Retired: 1992

(4) #5574-3

Victoria Station
Issued: 1989 • Current

(5) #5821-1

Whittlesbourne Church
Issued: 1994 • Current

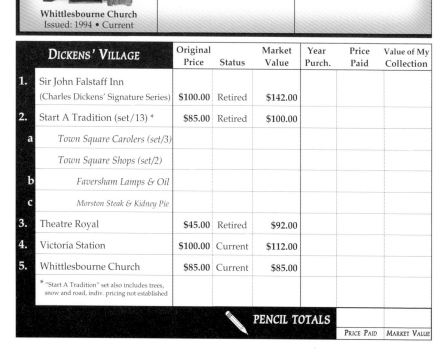

DICKENS' VILLAGE	Original Price	Status	Market Value	Year Purch.	Price Paid	Value of My Collection
1. Sir John Falstaff Inn (Charles Dickens' Signature Series)	$100.00	Retired	$142.00			
2. Start A Tradition (set/13) *	$85.00	Retired	$100.00			
a *Town Square Carolers (set/3)*						
Town Square Shops (set/2)						
b *Faversham Lamps & Oil*						
c *Morston Steak & Kidney Pie*						
3. Theatre Royal	$45.00	Retired	$92.00			
4. Victoria Station	$100.00	Current	$112.00			
5. Whittlesbourne Church	$85.00	Current	$85.00			
* "Start A Tradition" set also includes trees, snow and road, indiv. pricing not established						

✏ **PENCIL TOTALS**

	PRICE PAID	MARKET VALUE

1a #58331

Wrenbury Shops
The Chop Shop
Issued: 1995 • Current

1b #58331

Wrenbury Shops
T. Puddlewick Spectacle Shop
Issued: 1995 • Current

1c #58331

Wrenbury Shops
Wrenbury Baker
Issued: 1995 • Current

2a #5648-0

A. Bieler Farm
Pennsylvania Dutch Barn
(#56482)
Issued: 1993 • Retired: 1996

2b #5648-0

A. Bieler Farm
Pennsylvania Dutch Farmhouse
(#56481)
Issued: 1993 • Retired: 1996

3 #5940-4

Ada's Bed And Boarding House
Issued: 1988 • Retired: 1991

4 #56172

Apple Valley School
Issued: 1996 • Current

DICKENS' VILLAGE	Original Price	Status	Market Value	Year Purch.	Price Paid	Value of My Collection
1. Wrenbury Shops (set/3)	$100.00	Current	$100.00			
a *The Chop Shop*	$35.00		$35.00			
b *T. Puddlewick Spectacle Shop*	$35.00		$35.00			
c *Wrenbury Baker*	$35.00		$35.00			
NEW ENGLAND VILLAGE						
2. A. Bieler Farm (set/2)	$92.00	Retired	$112.00			
a *Pennsylvania Dutch Barn*	$50.00		$62.00			
b *Pennsylvania Dutch Farmhouse*	$42.00		$52.00			
3. Ada's Bed And Boarding House	$36.00	Retired	$320.00			
• Variation: Pale Yellow, rear steps attached separately			$136.00			
• Variation: Pale Yellow, rear steps part of mold			$163.00			
4. Apple Valley School	$35.00	Current	$35.00			

✏ **PENCIL TOTALS**

PRICE PAID	MARKET VALUE

	#5651-0		#5942-0		#5647-2
1		**2**		**3**	

Arlington Falls Church
Issued: 1994 • Current

Berkshire House
Issued: 1989 • Retired: 1991

Blue Star Ice Co.
Issued: 1993 • Current

4 #5642-1 — **Bluebird Seed And Bulb** Issued: 1992 • Retired: 1996

5 NEW! #56576 — **Bobwhite Cottage** Issued: 1996 • Current

6a #5657-0 — **Brewster Bay Cottages** *Jeremiah Brewster House* Issued: 1995 • Current

6b #5657-0 — **Brewster Bay Cottages** *Thomas T. Julian House* Issued: 1995 • Current

7 #5652-9 — **Cape Keag Fish Cannery** Issued: 1994 • Current

8 #5947-1 — **Captain's Cottage** Issued: 1990 • Retired: 1996

NEW ENGLAND VILLAGE	Original Price	Status	Market Value	Year Purch.	Price Paid	Value of My Collection
1. Arlington Falls Church	$42.00	Current	$42.00			
2. Berkshire House	$40.00	Retired	$157.00			
• Variation: Teal			$120.00			
3. Blue Star Ice Co.	$45.00	Current	$48.00			
4. Bluebird Seed and Bulb	$48.00	Retired	$60.00			
5. Bobwhite Cottage	$50.00	Current	$50.00			
6. Brewster Bay Cottages (set/2)	$90.00	Current	$90.00			
a *Jeremiah Brewster House*	$45.00		$45.00			
b *Thomas T. Julian House*	$45.00		$45.00			
7. Cape Keag Fish Cannery	$48.00	Current	$48.00			
8. Captain's Cottage	$40.00	Retired	$54.00			
			PENCIL TOTALS			
					PRICE PAID	MARKET VALUE

#5939-0

Cherry Lane Shops
Anne Shaw Toys
Issued: 1988 • Retired: 1990

#5939-0

Cherry Lane Shops
Ben's Barbershop
Issued: 1988 • Retired: 1990

#5939-0

Cherry Lane Shops
Otis Hayes Butcher Shop
Issued: 1988 • Retired: 1990

#56571

Chowder House
Issued: 1995 • Current

#5930-7

Craggy Cove Lighthouse
Issued: 1987 • Retired: 1994

NEW!

#56574

J. Hudson Stoveworks
Issued: 1996 • Current

#6538-2

Jacob Adams Farmhouse And Barn (set/5)
Issued: 1986 • Retired: 1989

#5944-7

Jannes Mullet Amish Barn
Issued: 1989 • Retired: 1992

#5943-9

Jannes Mullet Amish Farm House
Issued: 1989 • Retired: 1992

NEW ENGLAND VILLAGE	Original Price	Status	Market Value	Year Purch.	Price Paid	Value of My Collection
1. Cherry Lane Shops (set/3)	$80.00	Retired	$360.00			
a *Anne Shaw Toys*	$27.00		$175.00			
b *Ben's Barbershop*	$27.00		$115.00			
c *Otis Hayes Butcher Shop*	$27.00		$89.00			
2. Chowder House	$40.00	Current	$40.00			
3. Craggy Cove Lighthouse	$35.00	Retired	$74.00			
4. J. Hudson Stoveworks	$60.00	Current	$60.00			
5. Jacob Adams Farmhouse And Barn (set/5)	$65.00	Retired	$570.00			
6. Jannes Mullet Amish Barn	$48.00	Retired	$103.00			
7. Jannes Mullet Amish Farm House	$32.00	Retired	$122.00			
PENCIL TOTALS					PRICE PAID	MARKET VALUE

#5640-5

(1)

McGrebe-Cutters & Sleighs
Issued: 1991 • Retired: 1995

#56575

(2) NEW!

Navigational Charts & Maps
Issued: 1996 • Current

#6530-7

(3a)

New England Village
Apothecary Shop
Issued: 1986 • Retired: 1989

#6530-7

(3b)

New England Village
Brick Town Hall
Issued: 1986 • Retired: 1989

#6530-7

(3c)

New England Village
General Store
Issued: 1986 • Retired: 1989

#6530-7

(3d)

New England Village
Livery Stable & Boot Shop
Issued: 1986 • Retired: 1989

#6530-7

(3e)

New England Village
Nathaniel Bingham Fabrics
Issued: 1986 • Retired: 1989

#6530-7

(3f)

New England Village
Red Schoolhouse
Issued: 1986 • Retired: 1989

#6530-7

(3g)

New England Village
Steeple Church
Issued: 1986 • Retired: 1989

	NEW ENGLAND VILLAGE	Original Price	Status	Market Value	Year Purch.	Price Paid	Value of My Collection
1.	McGrebe–Cutters & Sleighs	$45.00	Retired	$72.00			
2.	Navigational Charts & Maps	$48.00	Current	$48.00			
3.	New England Village (set/7)	$170.00	Retired	$1280.00			
a	*Apothecary Shop*	$25.00		$113.00			
b	*Brick Town Hall*	$25.00		$220.00			
c	*General Store*	$25.00		$355.00			
d	*Livery Stable & Boot Shop*	$25.00		$152.00			
e	*Nathaniel Bingham Fabrics*	$25.00		$168.00			
f	*Red Schoolhouse*	$25.00		$280.00			
g	*Steeple Church* • Variation: tree attached w/glue	$25.00		$184.00 $106.00			

PENCIL TOTALS

	PRICE PAID	MARKET VALUE

#5932-3

(1) **Old North Church**
Issued: 1988 • Current

#56573

(2) **Pierce Boat Works**
Issued: 1995 • Current

#5653-7

(3) **Pigeonhead Lighthouse**
Issued: 1994 • Current

#5946-3

(4) **Shingle Creek House**
Issued: 1990 • Retired: 1994

#5954-4

(5a) **Sleepy Hollow**
Ichabod Crane's Cottage
Issued: 1990 • Retired: 1993

#5954-4

(5b) **Sleepy Hollow**
Sleepy Hollow School
Issued: 1990 • Retired: 1993

#5954-4

(5c) **Sleepy Hollow**
Van Tassel Manor
Issued: 1990 • Retired: 1993

#5955-2

(6) **Sleepy Hollow Church**
Issued: 1990 • Retired: 1993

#6543-9

(7) **Smythe Woolen Mill (LE-7,500)**
Issued: 1987 • Retired: 1988

	NEW ENGLAND VILLAGE	Original Price	Status	Market Value	Year Purch.	Price Paid	Value of My Collection
1.	Old North Church	$40.00	Current	$48.00			
2.	Pierce Boat Works	$55.00	Current	$55.00			
3.	Pigeonhead Lighthouse	$50.00	Current	$50.00			
4.	Shingle Creek House	$37.50	Retired	$65.00			
5.	Sleepy Hollow (set/3)	$96.00	Retired	$195.00			
a	*Ichabod Crane's Cottage*	$32.00		$65.00			
b	*Sleepy Hollow School*	$32.00		$100.00			
c	*Van Tassel Manor*	$32.00		$68.00			
6.	Sleepy Hollow Church	$36.00	Retired	$72.00			
7.	Smythe Woolen Mill (LE-7,500)	$42.00	Retired	$1180.00			

✎ **PENCIL TOTALS**

	PRICE PAID	MARKET VALUE

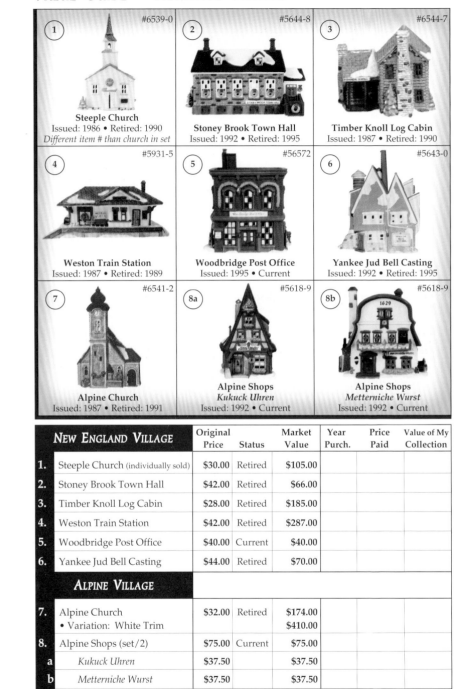

#6539-0

1

Steeple Church
Issued: 1986 • Retired: 1990
Different item # than church in set

#5644-8

2

Stoney Brook Town Hall
Issued: 1992 • Retired: 1995

#6544-7

3

Timber Knoll Log Cabin
Issued: 1987 • Retired: 1990

#5931-5

4

Weston Train Station
Issued: 1987 • Retired: 1989

#56572

5

Woodbridge Post Office
Issued: 1995 • Current

#5643-0

6

Yankee Jud Bell Casting
Issued: 1992 • Retired: 1995

#6541-2

7

Alpine Church
Issued: 1987 • Retired: 1991

#5618-9

8a

Alpine Shops
Kukuck Uhren
Issued: 1992 • Current

#5618-9

8b

Alpine Shops
Metterniche Wurst
Issued: 1992 • Current

	NEW ENGLAND VILLAGE	Original Price	Status	Market Value	Year Purch.	Price Paid	Value of My Collection
1.	Steeple Church (individually sold)	$30.00	Retired	$105.00			
2.	Stoney Brook Town Hall	$42.00	Retired	$66.00			
3.	Timber Knoll Log Cabin	$28.00	Retired	$185.00			
4.	Weston Train Station	$42.00	Retired	$287.00			
5.	Woodbridge Post Office	$40.00	Current	$40.00			
6.	Yankee Jud Bell Casting	$44.00	Retired	$70.00			
	ALPINE VILLAGE						
7.	Alpine Church • Variation: White Trim	$32.00	Retired	$174.00 $410.00			
8.	Alpine Shops (set/2)	$75.00	Current	$75.00			
a	*Kukuck Uhren*	$37.50		$37.50			
b	*Metterniche Wurst*	$37.50		$37.50			

✎ **PENCIL TOTALS**

PRICE PAID	MARKET VALUE

(1a) #6540-4

Alpine Village
Apotheke (#65407)
Issued: 1986 • Current

(1b) #6540-4

Alpine Village
Besson Bierkeller (#65405)
Issued: 1986 • Retired: 1996

(1c) #6540-4

Alpine Village
E. Staubr Backer (#65408)
Issued: 1986 • Current

(1d) #6540-4

Alpine Village
Gasthof Eisl (#65406)
Issued: 1986 • Retired: 1996

(1e) #6540-4

Alpine Village
Milch-Kase (#65409)
Issued: 1986 • Retired: 1996

(2) #5615-4

Bahnhof
Issued: 1990 • Retired: 1993

(3) #5614-6

Bakery & Chocolate Shop
Issued: 1994 • Current

(4) #56173

NEW!

Danube Music Publisher
Issued: 1996 • Current

(5) #5953-6

Grist Mill
Issued: 1988 • Current

	ALPINE VILLAGE	Original Price	Status	Market Value	Year Purch.	Price Paid	Value of My Collection
1.	Alpine Village (set/5)	$150.00	Retired	not established			
a	*Apotheke*	$25.00	Current	$39.00			
b	*Besson Bierkeller*	$25.00	Retired	$42.00			
c	*E. Staubr Backer*	$25.00	Current	$39.00			
d	*Gasthof Eisl*	$25.00	Retired	$42.00			
e	*Milch-Kase*	$25.00	Retired	$42.00			
2.	Bahnhof	$42.00	Retired	$84.00			
3.	Bakery & Chocolate Shop	$37.50	Current	$37.50			
4.	Danube Music Publisher	$55.00	Current	$55.00			
5.	Grist Mill	$42.00	Current	$45.00			

✎ **PENCIL TOTALS**

	PRICE PAID	MARKET VALUE

#5952-8	#56171	#5617-0
① Josef Engel Farmhouse Issued: 1987 • Retired: 1989	② Kamm Haus Issued: 1995 • Current	③ St. Nikolaus Kirche Issued: 1991 • Current
#5612-0	#5977-3	#5978-1
④ Sport Laden Issued: 1993 • Current	⑤ 5607 Park Avenue Townhouse Issued: 1989 • Retired: 1992	⑥ 5609 Park Avenue Townhouse Issued: 1989 • Retired: 1992
#5542-5	#5543-3	#58876
⑦ All Saints Corner Church Issued: 1991 • Current	⑧ Arts Academy Issued: 1991 • Retired: 1993	⑨ Brighton School Issued: 1995 • Current

	ALPINE VILLAGE	Original Price	Status	Market Value	Year Purch.	Price Paid	Value of My Collection
1.	Josef Engel Farmhouse	$33.00	Retired	$980.00			
2.	Kamm Haus	$42.00	Current	$42.00			
3.	St. Nikolaus Kirche	$37.50	Current	$37.50			
4.	Sport Laden	$50.00	Current	$50.00			
	CHRISTMAS IN THE CITY						
5.	5607 Park Avenue Townhouse	$48.00	Retired	$92.00			
6.	5609 Park Avenue Townhouse	$48.00	Retired	$91.00			
7.	All Saints Corner Church	$96.00	Current	$110.00			
8.	Arts Academy	$45.00	Retired	$85.00			
9.	Brighton School	$52.00	Current	$52.00			
				PENCIL TOTALS		PRICE PAID	MARKET VALUE

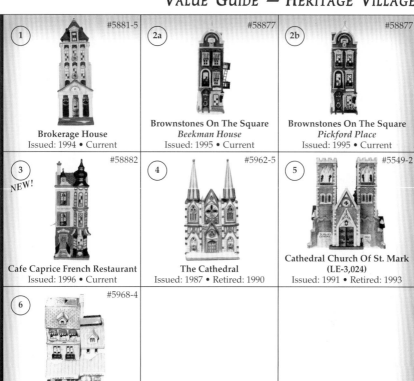

(1) #5881-5
Brokerage House
Issued: 1994 • Current

(2a) #58877
Brownstones On The Square
Beekman House
Issued: 1995 • Current

(2b) #58877
Brownstones On The Square
Pickford Place
Issued: 1995 • Current

(3) NEW! #58882
Cafe Caprice French Restaurant
Issued: 1996 • Current

(4) #5962-5
The Cathedral
Issued: 1987 • Retired: 1990

(5) #5549-2
Cathedral Church Of St. Mark
(LE-3,024)
Issued: 1991 • Retired: 1993

(6) #5968-4
Chocolate Shoppe
Issued: 1988 • Retired: 1991

CHRISTMAS IN THE CITY	Original Price	Status	Market Value	Year Purch.	Price Paid	Value of My Collection
1. Brokerage House	$48.00	Current	$48.00			
2. Brownstones On The Square (set/2)	$90.00	Current	$90.00			
a *Beekman House*	$45.00		$45.00			
b *Pickford Place*	$45.00		$45.00			
3. Cafe Caprice French Restaurant	$45.00	Current	$45.00			
4. The Cathedral	$60.00	Retired	$358.00			
5. Cathedral Church of St. Mark (LE-3,024)	$120.00	Retired	$2075.00			
6. Chocolate Shoppe	$40.00	Retired	$150.00			
		✏ PENCIL TOTALS				
					PRICE PAID	MARKET VALUE

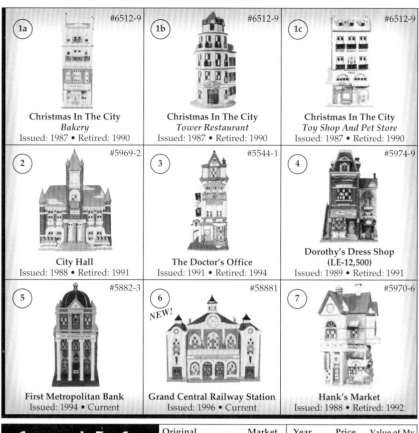

1a	#6512-9
Christmas In The City	
Bakery	
Issued: 1987 • Retired: 1990	

1b	#6512-9
Christmas In The City	
Tower Restaurant	
Issued: 1987 • Retired: 1990	

1c	#6512-9
Christmas In The City	
Toy Shop And Pet Store	
Issued: 1987 • Retired: 1990	

2	#5969-2
City Hall	
Issued: 1988 • Retired: 1991	

3	#5544-1
The Doctor's Office	
Issued: 1991 • Retired: 1994	

4	#5974-9
Dorothy's Dress Shop	
(LE-12,500)	
Issued: 1989 • Retired: 1991	

5	#5882-3
First Metropolitan Bank	
Issued: 1994 • Current	

6	#58881
NEW!	
Grand Central Railway Station	
Issued: 1996 • Current	

7	#5970-6
Hank's Market	
Issued: 1988 • Retired: 1992	

	CHRISTMAS IN THE CITY	Original Price	Status	Market Value	Year Purch.	Price Paid	Value of My Collection
1.	Christmas In The City (set/3)	$112.00	Retired	$560.00			
a	*Bakery*	$37.50		$110.00			
b	*Tower Restaurant*	$37.50		$247.00			
c	*Toy Shop And Pet Store*	$37.50		$250.00			
2.	City Hall	$65.00	Retired	$178.00			
3.	The Doctor's Office	$60.00	Retired	$88.00			
4.	Dorothy's Dress Shop (LE-12,500)	$70.00	Retired	$395.00			
5.	First Metropolitan Bank	$60.00	Current	$60.00			
6.	Grand Central Railway Station	$90.00	Current	$90.00			
7.	Hank's Market	$40.00	Retired	$84.00			
	✎ **PENCIL TOTALS**					PRICE PAID	MARKET VALUE

(1) #5883-1

Heritage Museum Of Art
Issued: 1994 • Current

(2) #5534-4

Hollydale's Department Store
Issued: 1991 • Current

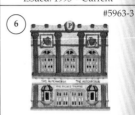

(3) #58875

Holy Name Church
Issued: 1995 • Current

(4) #5887-4

Ivy Terrace Apartments
Issued: 1995 • Current

(5) #5538-7

"Little Italy" Ristorante
Issued: 1991 • Retired: 1995

(6) #5963-3

Palace Theatre
Issued: 1987 • Retired: 1989

(7) #5536-0

Red Brick Fire Station
Issued: 1990 • Retired: 1995

(8) #5973-0

Ritz Hotel
Issued: 1989 • Retired: 1994

(9) #5961-7

Sutton Place Brownstones
Issued: 1987 • Retired: 1989

	CHRISTMAS IN THE CITY	Original Price	Status	Market Value	Year Purch.	Price Paid	Value of My Collection
1.	Heritage Museum Of Art	$96.00	Current	$96.00			
2.	Hollydale's Department Store	$75.00	Current	$85.00			
3.	Holy Name Church	$96.00	Current	$96.00			
4.	Ivy Terrace Apartments	$60.00	Current	$60.00			
5.	"Little Italy" Ristorante	$50.00	Retired	$83.00			
6.	Palace Theatre	$45.00	Retired	$960.00			
7.	Red Brick Fire Station	$55.00	Retired	$82.00			
8.	Ritz Hotel	$55.00	Retired	$85.00			
9.	Sutton Place Brownstones	$80.00	Retired	$900.00			
	PENCIL TOTALS					PRICE PAID	MARKET VALUE

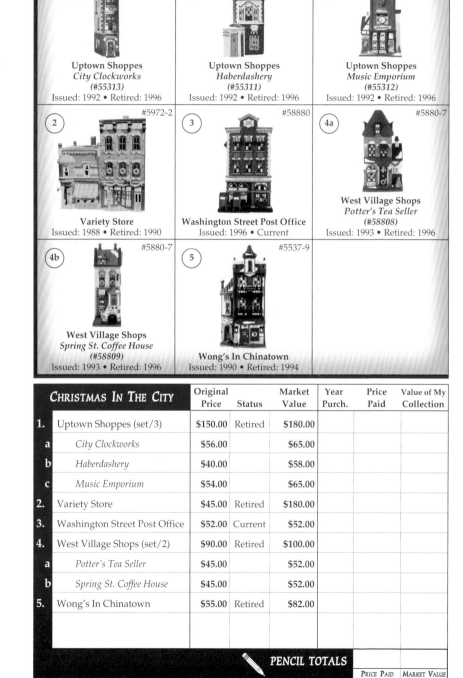

1a #5531-0

Uptown Shoppes
City Clockworks
(#55313)
Issued: 1992 • Retired: 1996

1b #5531-0

Uptown Shoppes
Haberdashery
(#55311)
Issued: 1992 • Retired: 1996

1c #5531-0

Uptown Shoppes
Music Emporium
(#55312)
Issued: 1992 • Retired: 1996

2 #5972-2

Variety Store
Issued: 1988 • Retired: 1990

3 #58880

Washington Street Post Office
Issued: 1996 • Current

4a #5880-7

West Village Shops
Potter's Tea Seller
(#58808)
Issued: 1993 • Retired: 1996

4b #5880-7

West Village Shops
Spring St. Coffee House
(#58809)
Issued: 1993 • Retired: 1996

5 #5537-9

Wong's In Chinatown
Issued: 1990 • Retired: 1994

	CHRISTMAS IN THE CITY	Original Price	Status	Market Value	Year Purch.	Price Paid	Value of My Collection
1.	Uptown Shoppes (set/3)	$150.00	Retired	$180.00			
a	*City Clockworks*	$56.00		$65.00			
b	*Haberdashery*	$40.00		$58.00			
c	*Music Emporium*	$54.00		$65.00			
2.	Variety Store	$45.00	Retired	$180.00			
3.	Washington Street Post Office	$52.00	Current	$52.00			
4.	West Village Shops (set/2)	$90.00	Retired	$100.00			
a	*Potter's Tea Seller*	$45.00		$52.00			
b	*Spring St. Coffee House*	$45.00		$52.00			
5.	Wong's In Chinatown	$55.00	Retired	$82.00			
				✏ PENCIL TOTALS			
						PRICE PAID	MARKET VALUE

#5634-0	#56393	#5625-1
①	**② NEW!**	**③**
Beard Barber Shop Issued: 1994 • Current	**Christmas Bread Bakers** Issued: 1996 • Current	**Elfie's Sleds & Skates** Issued: 1992 • Retired: 1996

#56384	#5633-2	#56387
④	**⑤**	**⑥**
Elfin Forge & Assembly Shop Issued: 1995 • Current	**Elfin Snow Cone Works** Issued: 1994 • Current	**Elves' Trade School** Issued: 1995 • Current

#56392	#5620-0
⑦ NEW!	**⑧**
Hall of Records Issued: 1996 • Current	**Neenee's Dolls & Toys** Issued: 1991 • Retired: 1995

NORTH POLE		Original Price	Status	Market Value	Year Purch.	Price Paid	Value of My Collection
1.	Beard Barber Shop	$27.50	Current	$27.50			
2.	Christmas Bread Bakers	$55.00	Current	$55.00			
3.	Elfie's Sleds & Skates	$48.00	Retired	$69.00			
4.	Elfin Forge & Assembly Shop	$65.00	Current	$65.00			
5.	Elfin Snow Cone Works	$40.00	Current	$40.00			
6.	Elves' Trade School	$50.00	Current	$50.00			
7.	Hall of Records	$50.00	Current	$50.00			
8.	Neenee's Dolls & Toys	$37.50	Retired	$65.00			

PENCIL TOTALS

PRICE PAID	MARKET VALUE

#5601-4 (1a)

North Pole
Elf Bunkhouse (#56016)
Issued: 1990 • Retired: 1996

#5601-4 (1b)

North Pole
Reindeer Barn (#56015)
Issued: 1990 • Current

#5626-0 (2)

North Pole Chapel
Issued: 1993 • Current

#5635-9 (3)

**North Pole Dolls
& Santa's Bear Works (set/3)**
Issued: 1994 • Current

#5627-8 (4)

North Pole Express Depot
Issued: 1993 • Current

#5621-9 (5a)

North Pole Shops
Orly's Bell & Harness Supply
Issued: 1991 • Retired: 1995

#5621-9 (5b)

North Pole Shops
Rimpy's Bakery
Issued: 1991 • Retired: 1995

#5624-3 (6)

**Obbie's Books
& Letrinka's Candy**
Issued: 1992 • Retired: 1996

NORTH POLE	Original Price	Status	Market Value	Year Purch.	Price Paid	Value of My Collection
1. North Pole (set/2)	$70.00	Retired	not established			
a *Elf Bunkhouse*	$35.00	Retired	$50.00			
b *Reindeer Barn*	$35.00	Current	$40.00			
2. North Pole Chapel	$45.00	Current	$45.00			
3. North Pole Dolls & Santa's Bear Works (set/3)	$96.00	Current	$96.00			
Entrance						
North Pole Dolls						
Santa's Bear Works						
4. North Pole Express Depot	$48.00	Current	$48.00			
5. North Pole Shops (set/2)	$75.00	Retired	$125.00			
a *Orly's Bell & Harness Shop*	$37.50		$65.00			
b *Rimpy's Bakery*	$37.50		$65.00			
6. Obbie's Books & Letrinka's Candy	$70.00	Retired	$95.00			

✎ **PENCIL TOTALS**

	PRICE PAID	MARKET VALUE

#56388
1
Popcorn & Cranberry House
Issued: 1996 • Current

#5623-5
2
Post Office
Issued: 1992 • Current

#56391
3
NEW!
Route 1, North Pole, Home Of
Mr. & Mrs. Claus
Issued: 1996 • Current

#56389
4
Santa's Bell Repair
Issued: 1996 • Current

#5629-4
5
Santa's Lookout Tower
Issued: 1993 • Current

#56386
6
Santa's Rooming House
Issued: 1995 • Current

#5628-6
7
Santa's Woodworks
Issued: 1993 • Retired: 1996

#5600-6
8
Santa's Workshop
Issued: 1990 • Retired: 1993

	NORTH POLE	Original Price	Status	Market Value	Year Purch.	Price Paid	Value of My Collection
1.	Popcorn & Cranberry House	$45.00	Current	$45.00			
2.	Post Office	$45.00	Current	$50.00			
3.	Route 1, North Pole, Home Of Mr. & Mrs. Claus	$110.00	Current	$110.00			
4.	Santa's Bell Repair	$45.00	Current	$45.00			
5.	Santa's Lookout Tower	$45.00	Current	$48.00			
6.	Santa's Rooming House	$50.00	Current	$50.00			
7.	Santa's Woodworks	$42.00	Retired	$60.00			
8.	Santa's Workshop	$72.00	Retired	$525.00			
	PENCIL TOTALS					PRICE PAID	MARKET VALUE

1a #56390

Start A Tradition (set/12)
Candy Cane Elves
(set/2, accessory)
Issued: 1996 • Retired: 1996

1b #56390

Start A Tradition (set/12)
Candy Cane & Peppermint Shop
Issued: 1996 • Retired: 1996

1c #56390

Start A Tradition (set/12)
Gift Wrap & Ribbons
Issued: 1996 • Retired: 1996

2 #5622-7

Tassy's Mittens
& Hassel's Woolies
Issued: 1991 • Retired: 1995

3 #5638-3

Tin Soldier Shop
Issued: 1995 • Current

4 #56385

Weather & Time Observatory
Issued: 1995 • Current

	NORTH POLE	Original Price	Status	Market Value	Year Purch.	Price Paid	Value of My Collection
1.	Start A Tradition (set/12)	$85.00	Retired	$120.00			
a	*Candy Cane Elves (set/2)*						
b	*Candy Cane & Peppermint Shop*						
c	*Gift Wrap & Ribbons*						
2.	Tassy's Mittens & Hassel's Woolies	$50.00	Retired	$88.00			
3.	Tin Soldier Shop	$42.00	Current	$42.00			
4.	Weather & Time Observatory	$50.00	Current	$50.00			
	✎ PENCIL TOTALS					PRICE PAID	MARKET VALUE

#5352-0

① Disneyland Fire Department #105
Issued: 1994 • Retired: 1996

#5350-3

② Mickey's Christmas Carol (set/2)
Issued: 1994 • Retired: 1996

#5351-1

③a Olde World Antiques Shops
Olde World Antiques I
Issued: 1994 • Retired: 1996

#5351-1

③b Olde World Antiques Shops
Olde World Antiques II
Issued: 1994 • Retired: 1996

#53521

④ Silversmith
Issued: 1995 • Retired: 1996

#53522

⑤ Tinker Bell's Treasures
Issued: 1995 • Retired: 1996

#5975-7

⑥ Little Town Of Bethlehem
(set/12)
Issued: 1987 • Current

DISNEY PARKS VILLAGE SERIES		Original Price	Status	Market Value	Year Purch.	Price Paid	Value of My Collection
1.	Disneyland Fire Department #105	$45.00	Retired	$54.00	1997	600 w/ all accessories	
2.	Mickey's Christmas Carol (set/2)	$144.00	Retired	$170.00			
3.	Olde World Antiques Shops (set/2)	$90.00	Retired	$105.00			
a	*Olde World Antiques I*	$45.00		$59.00			
b	*Olde World Antiques II*	$45.00		$59.00			
4.	Silversmith	$50.00	Retired	$200.00			
5.	Tinker Bell's Treasures	$60.00	Retired	$210.00			
LITTLE TOWN OF BETHLEHEM						600	739+13/1870
6.	Little Town Of Bethlehem (set/12)	$150.00	Current	$150.00			
				✏ PENCIL TOTALS		PRICE PAID	MARKET VALUE

Use this page to record future Heritage Village buildings.

Heritage Village	Original Price	Status	Market Value	Year Purch.	Price Paid	Value of My Collection
PENCIL TOTALS					Price Paid	Market Value

1	#5866-1	Christmas At The Park (set/3) Issued: 1993 • Current
2	#98711	Christmas Bells (Special Event Piece) Issued: 1996 • Retired: 1996
3	#5807-6	Churchyard Fence Extensions (set/4) Issued: 1992 • Current
4	#5563-8	Churchyard Fence Gate (set/3) Issued: 1992 • Retired: 1992
5	#5806-8	Churchyard Gate And Fence (set/3) Issued: 1992 • Current
6	#5820-3	Dashing Through The Snow Issued: 1993 • Current
7	#5530-1	Gate House (LE-1992) Issued: 1992 • Retired: 1992 *Special Event Piece*
8	#9953-8	Heritage Village Promotional Sign Issued: 1989 • Retired: 1990
9	#6510-2	Lighted Tree w/Children And Ladder (set/3) Issued: 1986 • Retired: 1989

ACCESSORIES
GENERAL HERITAGE VILLAGE

	ACCESSORIES GENERAL HERITAGE VILLAGE	Original Price	Status	Market Value	Year Purch.	Price Paid	Value of My Collection
1.	Christmas At The Park (set/3)	$27.50	Current	$27.50			
2.	Christmas Bells (Special Event Piece)	$35.00	Retired	$55.00			
3.	Churchyard Fence Extensions (set/4)	$16.00	Current	$16.00			
4.	Churchyard Fence Gate (set/3)	$15.00	Retired	$48.00			
5.	Churchyard Gate And Fence (set/3)	$15.00	Current	$15.00			
6.	Dashing Through The Snow	$32.50	Current	$32.50			
7.	Gate House (LE-1992)	$22.50	Retired	$68.00			
8.	Heritage Village Promotional Sign	$5.00	Retired	$25.00			
9.	Lighted Tree w/Children And Ladder (set/3)	$35.00	Retired	$350.00			

PENCIL TOTALS

	PRICE PAID	MARKET VALUE

Value Guide — Heritage Village

#5982-0
(1) One Horse Open Sleigh
Issued: 1988 • Retired: 1993

#5556-5
(2) Playing In The Snow (set/3)
Issued: 1993 • Retired: 1996

#6537-4
(3) Porcelain Trees (set/2)
Issued: 1986 • Retired: 1992

#5523-9
(4) Skating Party (set/3)
Issued: 1991 • Current

#6545-5
(5) Skating Pond
Issued: 1987 • Retired: 1990

#5938-2
(6) Snow Children (set/3)
Issued: 1988 • Retired: 1994

#5513-1
(7) Town Square Gazebo
Issued: 1989 • Current

#5565-4
(8) Town Tree (set/5)
Issued: 1993 • Current

#5566-2
(9) Town Tree Trimmers (set/4)
Issued: 1993 • Current

	ACCESSORIES GENERAL HERITAGE VILLAGE	Original Price	Status	Market Value	Year Purch.	Price Paid	Value of My Collection
1.	One Horse Open Sleigh	$20.00	Retired	$39.00			
2.	Playing In The Snow (set/3)	$25.00	Retired	$32.00			
3.	Porcelain Trees (set/2)	$14.00	Retired	$38.00			
4.	Skating Party (set/3)	$27.50	Current	$27.50			
5.	Skating Pond	$24.00	Retired	$85.00			
6.	Snow Children (set/3)	$15.00	Retired	$30.00			
7.	Town Square Gazebo	$19.00	Current	$19.00			
8.	Town Tree (set/5)	$45.00	Current	$45.00			
9.	Town Tree Trimmers (set/4)	$32.50	Current	$32.50			
	PENCIL TOTALS					PRICE PAID	MARKET VALUE

#5656-1	#52593	#52642
① Two Rivers Bridge Issued: 1994 • Current	**②** Up, Up & Away Issued: 1995 • Current	**③** NEW! Village Animated Accessory Track Issued: 1996 • Current
#5247-7	#5229-9	#52641
④ Village Animated All Around The Park (set/18) Issued: 1994 • Retired: 1996	**⑤** Village Animated Skating Pond (set/15) Issued: 1993 • Current	**⑥** NEW! Village Animated Ski Moutain Issued: 1996 • Current
#5997-8	#5980-3	
⑦ Village Express Train (set/22) Issued: 1987 • Retired: 1988 *Black train manufactured by Tyco*	**⑧** Village Express Train (set/22) Issued: 1988 • Retired: 1996 *Red, silver & black train manufactured by Bachman Trains*	

	ACCESSORIES GENERAL HERITAGE VILLAGE	Original Price	Status	Market Value	Year Purch.	Price Paid	Value of My Collection
1.	Two Rivers Bridge	$35.00	Current	$35.00			
2.	Up, Up & Away	$40.00	Current	$40.00			
3.	Village Animated Accessory Track	$65.00	Current	$65.00			
4.	Village Animated All Around The Park (set/18)	$95.00	Retired	$102.00			
5.	Village Animated Skating Pond (set/15)	$60.00	Current	$60.00			
6.	Village Animated Ski Mountain	$75.00	Current	$75.00			
7.	Village Express Train (set/22)	$90.00	Retired	$315.00			
8.	Village Express Train (set/22)	$95.00	Retired	$110.00			
	✎ PENCIL TOTALS					PRICE PAID	MARKET VALUE

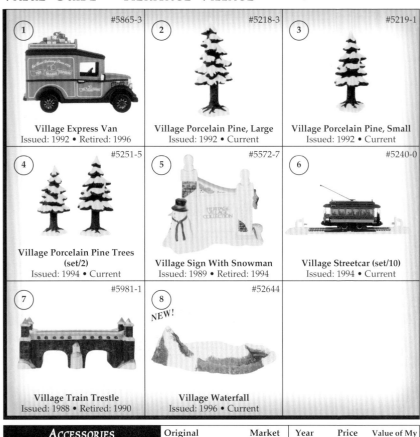

#5865-3	#5218-3	#5219-1
Village Express Van Issued: 1992 • Retired: 1996	**Village Porcelain Pine, Large** Issued: 1992 • Current	**Village Porcelain Pine, Small** Issued: 1992 • Current
#5251-5	#5572-7	#5240-0
Village Porcelain Pine Trees (set/2) Issued: 1994 • Current	**Village Sign With Snowman** Issued: 1989 • Retired: 1994	**Village Streetcar (set/10)** Issued: 1994 • Current
#5981-1	#52644 NEW!	
Village Train Trestle Issued: 1988 • Retired: 1990	**Village Waterfall** Issued: 1996 • Current	

	ACCESSORIES GENERAL HERITAGE VILLAGE	Original Price	Status	Market Value	Year Purch.	Price Paid	Value of My Collection
1.	Village Express Van (green)	**$25.00**	Retired	**$30.00**			
	• Variations: Black – $154; Gold – $1,100; Bachman's – $95; Bronner's Christmas Wonderland – $65; Canadian – $75; The Christmas Dove – $65; European Imports – $65; Fortunoff – $140; The Incredible Christmas Place (Pigeon Forge) – $85; Lemon Tree – $65; The Limited Edition – $105; Lock Stock & Barrel – $135; North Pole City – $65; Parkwest – not established; Robert's Christmas Wonderland – $65; St. Nick's – $80; Stats – $60; William Glen – $65; The Windsor Shoppe – $65.						
2.	Village Porcelain Pine, Large	**$12.50**	Current	**$12.50**			
3.	Village Porcelain Pine, Small	**$10.00**	Current	**$10.00**			
4.	Village Porcelain Pine Trees (set/2)	**$15.00**	Current	**$15.00**			
5.	Village Sign w/Snowman	**$10.00**	Retired	**$22.00**			
6.	Village Streetcar (set/10)	**$65.00**	Current	**$65.00**			
7.	Village Train Trestle	**$17.00**	Retired	**$75.00**			
8.	Village Waterfall	**$65.00**	Current	**$65.00**			

✎ **PENCIL TOTALS**

	PRICE PAID	MARKET VALUE

#5803-3

(1) The Bird Seller (set/3)
Issued: 1992 • Retired: 1995

#5934-0

(2) Blacksmith (set/3)
Issued: 1987 • Retired: 1990

#5819-0

(3) Bringing Fleeces To The Mill (set/2)
Issued: 1993 • Current

#5558-1

(4) Bringing Home The Yule Log (set/3)
Issued: 1991 • Current

#58390

(5) Brixton Road Watchman (set/2)
Issued: 1995 • Current

#5818-1

(6) C. Bradford, Wheelwright & Son (set/2)
Issued: 1993 • Retired: 1996

#6526-9

(7) Carolers (set/3)
Issued: 1984 • Retired: 1990

#5570-0

(8) Carolers On The Doorstep (set/4)
Issued: 1990 • Retired: 1993

#58396

(9) Caroling With The Cratchit Family, Revisited (set/3)
Issued: 1996 • Current

ACCESSORIES DICKENS' VILLAGE

	ACCESSORIES DICKENS' VILLAGE	Original Price	Status	Market Value	Year Purch.	Price Paid	Value of My Collection
1.	The Bird Seller (set/3)	$25.00	Retired	$32.00			
2.	Blacksmith (set/3)	$20.00	Retired	$82.00			
3.	Bringing Fleeces To The Mill (set/2)	$35.00	Current	$35.00			
4.	Bringing Home The Yule Log (set/3)	$27.50	Current	$28.00			
5.	Brixton Road Watchman (set/2)	$25.00	Current	$25.00			
6.	C. Bradford, Wheelwright & Son (set/2)	$24.00	Retired	$29.00			
7.	Carolers (set/3) • Variation: white lamp post	$10.00	Retired	$43.00 $125.00			
8.	Carolers On The Doorstep (set/4)	$25.00	Retired	$46.00			
9.	Caroling With The Cratchit Family, Revisited (set/3)	$37.50	Current	$37.50			

✏️ **PENCIL TOTALS**

	PRICE PAID	MARKET VALUE

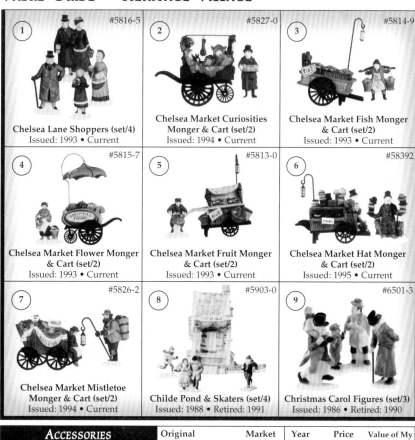

1	#5816-5	2	#5827-0	3	#5814-9
Chelsea Lane Shoppers (set/4) Issued: 1993 • Current		**Chelsea Market Curiosities Monger & Cart (set/2)** Issued: 1994 • Current		**Chelsea Market Fish Monger & Cart (set/2)** Issued: 1993 • Current	
4	#5815-7	5	#5813-0	6	#58392
Chelsea Market Flower Monger & Cart (set/2) Issued: 1993 • Current		**Chelsea Market Fruit Monger & Cart (set/2)** Issued: 1993 • Current		**Chelsea Market Hat Monger & Cart (set/2)** Issued: 1995 • Current	
7	#5826-2	8	#5903-0	9	#6501-3
Chelsea Market Mistletoe Monger & Cart (set/2) Issued: 1994 • Current		**Childe Pond & Skaters (set/4)** Issued: 1988 • Retired: 1991		**Christmas Carol Figures (set/3)** Issued: 1986 • Retired: 1990	

	ACCESSORIES DICKENS' VILLAGE	Original Price	Status	Market Value	Year Purch.	Price Paid	Value of My Collection
1.	Chelsea Lane Shoppers (set/4)	$30.00	Current	$30.00			
2.	Chelsea Market Curiosities Monger & Cart (set/2)	$27.50	Current	$27.50			
3.	Chelsea Market Fish Monger & Cart (set/2)	$25.00	Current	$25.00			
4.	Chelsea Market Flower Monger & Cart (set/2)	$27.50	Current	$27.50			
5.	Chelsea Market Fruit Monger & Cart (set/2)	$25.00	Current	$25.00			
6.	Chelsea Market Hat Monger & Cart (set/2)	$27.50	Current	$27.50			
7.	Chelsea Market Mistletoe Monger & Cart (set/2)	$25.00	Current	$25.00			
8.	Childe Pond & Skaters (set/4)	$30.00	Retired	$92.00			
9.	Christmas Carol Figures (set/3)	$12.50	Retired	$92.00			

✎ **PENCIL TOTALS**

PRICE PAID	MARKET VALUE

	Original Price	Status	Market Value	Year Purch.	Price Paid	Value of My Collection
ACCESSORIES DICKENS' VILLAGE						
1. Christmas Carol Holiday Trimming Set (set/21)	$65.00	Current	$65.00			
2. "A Christmas Carol" Reading By Charles Dickens (set/4)	$45.00	Current	$45.00			
3. "A Christmas Carol" Reading By Charles Dickens (set/7, LE-42,500)	$75.00	Current	$75.00			
4. Christmas Morning Figures (set/3)	$18.00	Current	$18.00			
5. Christmas Spirits Figures (set/4)	$27.50	Current	$27.50			
6. Cobbler & Clock Peddler (set/2)	$25.00	Current	$25.00			
7. Come Into The Inn (set/3)	$22.00	Retired	$30.00			
8. Constables (set/3)	$17.50	Retired	$67.00			
9. Crown & Cricket Inn Ornament	$15.00	Retired	$22.00			
PENCIL TOTALS					PRICE PAID	MARKET VALUE

1. #5551-4 — **David Copperfield Characters (set/5)** — Issued: 1989 • Retired: 1992

2. #9872-8 — **Dedlock Arms Ornament** — Issued: 1994 • Retired: 1994

3. #6569-2 — **Dickens' Village Sign** — Issued: 1987 • Retired: 1993

4. #6590-0 — **Dover Coach** — Issued: 1987 • Retired: 1990

5. #58384 — NEW! — **Eight Maids-A-Milking** — Issued: 1996 • Current — *The Twelve Days Of Dickens' Village*

6. #5805-0 — **English Post Box** — Issued: 1992 • Current

7. #5901-3 — **Farm People & Animals (set/5)** — Issued: 1987 • Retired: 1989

8. #5928-5 — **Fezziwig & Friends (set/3)** — Issued: 1988 • Retired: 1990

9. #58400 — NEW! — **The Fezziwig Delivery Wagon (Christmas Carol Revisited)** — Issued: 1996 • Current

	ACCESSORIES DICKENS' VILLAGE	Original Price	Status	Market Value	Year Purch.	Price Paid	Value of My Collection
1.	David Copperfield Characters (set/5)	$32.50	Retired	$49.00			
2.	Dedlock Arms Ornament	$12.50	Retired	$24.00			
3.	Dickens' Village Sign	$6.00	Retired	$20.00			
4.	Dover Coach	$18.00	Retired	$74.00			
	• Variation: w/out mustache			$107.00			
5.	Eight Maids-A-Milking *(The Twelve Days Of Dickens' Village)*	$25.00	Current	$25.00			
6.	English Post Box	$4.50	Current	$4.50			
7.	Farm People & Animals (set/5)	$24.00	Retired	$100.00			
8.	Fezziwig & Friends (set/3)	$12.50	Retired	$56.00			
9.	The Fezziwig Delivery Wagon (Christmas Carol Revisited)	$32.50	Current	$32.50			

✏️ **PENCIL TOTALS**

PRICE PAID	MARKET VALUE

#58381
1
Five Golden Rings (set/2)
Issued: 1995 • Current
The Twelve Days Of Dickens' Village

#5573-5
2
The Flying Scot Train (set/4)
Issued: 1990 • Current

#58379
3
Four Calling Birds (set/2)
Issued: 1995 • Current
The Twelve Days Of Dickens' Village

#58402
4
NEW!
Gingerbread Vendor (set/2)
Issued: 1996 • Current

#98729
5
The Grapes Inn Ornament
Issued: 1996 • Retired: 1996

#5561-1
6
Holiday Coach
Issued: 1991 • Current

#5571-9
7
Holiday Travelers (set/3)
Issued: 1990 • Current

#5581-6
8
King's Road Cab
Issued: 1989 • Current

#5577-8
9
Lamplighter w/Lamp (set/2)
Issued: 1989 • Current

ACCESSORIES
DICKENS' VILLAGE

	ACCESSORIES DICKENS' VILLAGE	Original Price	Status	Market Value	Year Purch.	Price Paid	Value of My Collection
1.	Five Golden Rings (set/2, *The Twelve Days Of Dickens' Village*)	$27.50	Current	$27.50			
2.	The Flying Scot Train (set/4)	$48.00	Current	$50.00			
3.	Four Calling Birds (set/2, *The Twelve Days Of Dickens' Village*)	$32.50	Current	$32.50			
4.	Gingerbread Vendor (set/2)	$22.50	Current	$22.50			
5.	The Grapes Inn Ornament	$15.00	Retired	$22.00			
6.	Holiday Coach	$68.00	Current	$70.00			
7.	Holiday Travelers (set/3)	$22.50	Current	$25.00			
8.	King's Road Cab	$30.00	Current	$30.00			
9.	Lamplighter w/Lamp (set/2)	$9.00	Current	$10.00			

PENCIL TOTALS

PRICE PAID	MARKET VALUE

1. **Lionhead Bridge**
Issued: 1992 • Current
#5864-5

2. **Nicholas Nickleby Characters (set/4)**
Issued: 1988 • Retired: 1991
#5929-3

3. **The Old Puppeteer (set/3)**
Issued: 1992 • Retired: 1995
#5802-5

4. **Oliver Twist Characters (set/3)**
Issued: 1991 • Retired: 1993
#5554-9

5. **Ox Sled**
Issued: 1987 • Retired: 1989
#5951-0

6. **A Partridge In A Pear Tree**
Issued: 1995 • Current
#5835-1

7. **A Peaceful Glow On Christmas Eve (set/3)**
Issued: 1994 • Current
#5830-0

8. **The Pied Bull Inn Ornament**
Issued: 1996 • Retired: 1996
#98731

9. **Portobello Road Peddlers (set/3)**
Issued: 1994 • Current
#5828-9

	ACCESSORIES DICKENS' VILLAGE	Original Price	Status	Market Value	Year Purch.	Price Paid	Value of My Collection
1.	Lionhead Bridge	$22.00	Current	$22.00			
2.	Nicholas Nickleby Characters (set/4)	$20.00	Retired	$41.00			
3.	The Old Puppeteer (set/3)	$32.00	Retired	$43.00			
4.	Oliver Twist Characters (set/3)	$35.00	Retired	$49.00			
5.	Ox Sled	$20.00	Retired	$147.00			
	• Variation: tan pants, green seat			$263.00			
6.	A Partridge In A Pear Tree *(The Twelve Days Of Dickens' Village)*	$35.00	Current	$35.00			
7.	A Peaceful Glow On Christmas Eve (set/3)	$30.00	Current	$30.00			
8.	The Pied Bull Inn Ornament	$15.00	Retired	$20.00			
9.	Portobello Road Peddlers (set/3)	$27.50	Current	$27.50			
			PENCIL TOTALS			PRICE PAID	MARKET VALUE

#9871-0 (1)  **Postern** Issued: 1994 • Retired: 1994 *10 Year Anniversary Piece*	#5559-0 (2)  **Poultry Market (set/3)** Issued: 1991 • Retired: 1995	#58401 (3) NEW!  **Red Christmas Sulky** Issued: 1996 • Current
#5578-6 (4)  **Royal Coach** Issued: 1989 • Retired: 1992	#58383 (5) NEW!  **Seven Swans-A-Swimming** Issued: 1996 • Current *The Twelve Days Of Dickens' Village*	#5966-8 (6)  **Shopkeepers (set/4)** Issued: 1987 • Retired: 1988
#5950-1 (7)  **Silo & Hay Shed (set/2)** Issued: 1987 • Retired: 1989	#9870-1 (8)  **Sir John Falstaff Inn Ornament** Issued: 1995 • Retired: 1995	#58382 (9)  **Six Geese A-Laying (set/2)** Issued: 1995 • Current *The Twelve Days Of Dickens' Village*

ACCESSORIES — DICKENS' VILLAGE (side tab)

	ACCESSORIES DICKENS' VILLAGE	Original Price	Status	Market Value	Year Purch.	Price Paid	Value of My Collection
1.	Postern (10 Year Anniversary Piece)	$17.50	Retired	$30.00			
2.	Poultry Market (set/3)	$30.00	Retired	$42.00			
3.	Red Christmas Sulky	$30.00	Current	$30.00			
4.	Royal Coach	$55.00	Retired	$82.00			
5.	Seven Swans-A-Swimming *(The Twelve Days Of Dickens' Village)*	$27.50	Current	$27.50			
6.	Shopkeepers (set/4)	$15.00	Retired	$42.00			
7.	Silo & Hay Shed (set/2)	$18.00	Retired	$175.00			
8.	Sir John Falstaff Inn Ornament	$15.00	Retired	$22.00			
9.	Six Geese A-Laying (set/2, *The Twelve Days Of Dickens' Village*)	$30.00	Current	$30.00			

✎ **PENCIL TOTALS**

PRICE PAID	MARKET VALUE

1 #6546-3
Stone Bridge
Issued: 1987 • Retired: 1990

2 #58391
"Tallyho!" (set/5)
Issued: 1995 • Current

3 #58395
Tending New Calves With Kids (set/3)
Issued: 1996 • Current

4 #5829-7
Thatchers (set/3)
Issued: 1994 • Current

5 #58378
Three French Hens (set/3)
Issued: 1995 • Current
The Twelve Days Of Dickens' Village

6 #5569-7
Town Crier & Chimney Sweep (set/2)
Issued: 1990 • Current

7 #5836-0
Two Turtle Doves (set/4)
Issued: 1995 • Current
The Twelve Days Of Dickens' Village

8 #5575-1
Victoria Station Train Platform
Issued: 1990 • Current

9 #5804-1
Village Street Peddlers (set/2)
Issued: 1992 • Retired: 1994

	ACCESSORIES DICKENS' VILLAGE	Original Price	Status	Market Value	Year Purch.	Price Paid	Value of My Collection
1.	Stone Bridge	$12.00	Retired	$91.00			
2.	"Tallyho!" (set/5)	$50.00	Current	$50.00			
3.	Tending New Calves With Kids (set/3)	$30.00	Current	$30.00			
4.	Thatchers (set/3)	$35.00	Current	$35.00			
5.	Three French Hens (set/3, *The Twelve Days Of Dickens' Village*)	$32.50	Current	$32.50			
6.	Town Crier & Chimney Sweep (set/2)	$15.00	Current	$16.00			
7.	Two Turtle Doves (set/4, *The Twelve Days Of Dickens' Village*)	$32.50	Current	$32.50			
8.	Victoria Station Train Platform	$20.00	Current	$22.00			
9.	Village Street Peddlers (set/2)	$16.00	Retired	$28.00			
	✎ PENCIL TOTALS					PRICE PAID	MARKET VALUE

#6527-7
1

#6547-1
2

#5580-8
3

Village Train (set/3)
Issued: 1985 • Retired: 1986

Village Well & Holy Cross (set/2)
Issued: 1987 • Retired: 1989

**Violet Vendor/Carolers/
Chestnut Vendor (set/3)**
Issued: 1989 • Retired: 1992

#5817-3
4

#5825-4
5

#58393
6

**Vision Of A Christmas
Past (set/3)**
Issued: 1993 • Retired: 1996

Winter Sleighride
Issued: 1994 • Current

**"Ye Olde Lamplighter"
Dickens' Village Sign**
Issued: 1995 • Current

#58397
7

#5949-8
8

#5948-0
9

Yeoman Of The Guard (set/5)
Issued: 1996 • Current

Amish Buggy
Issued: 1990 • Retired: 1992

Amish Family (set/3)
Issued: 1990 • Retired: 1992

	ACCESSORIES DICKENS' VILLAGE	Original Price	Status	Market Value	Year Purch.	Price Paid	Value of My Collection
1.	Village Train (set/3)	$12.00	Retired	$450.00			
2.	Village Well & Holy Cross (set/2)	$13.00	Retired	$168.00			
3.	Violet Vendor/Carolers/ Chestnut Vendor (set/3)	$23.00	Retired	$44.00			
4.	Vision Of A Christmas Past (set/3)	$27.50	Retired	$32.00			
5.	Winter Sleighride	$18.00	Current	$18.00			
6.	"Ye Olde Lamplighter" Dickens' Village Sign	$20.00	Current	$20.00			
7.	Yeoman Of The Guard (set/5)	$30.00	Current	$30.00			
	ACCESSORIES NEW ENGLAND VILLAGE						
8.	Amish Buggy	$22.00	Retired	$57.00			
9.	Amish Family (set/3)	$20.00	Retired	$40.00			
	• Variation: father w/mustache			$60.00			

PENCIL TOTALS

	PRICE PAID	MARKET VALUE

#5650-2
(1)
Blue Star Ice Harvesters (set/2)
Issued: 1993 • Current

#56594
(2) NEW!
Christmas Bazaar . . .
Handmade Quilts (set/2)
Issued: 1996 • Current

#56595
(3) NEW!
Christmas Bazaar . . . Woolens
& Preserves (set/2)
Issued: 1996 • Current

#6531-5
(4)
Covered Wooden Bridge
Issued: 1986 • Retired: 1990

#5945-5
(5)
Farm Animals (set/4)
Issued: 1989 • Retired: 1991

#56588
(6)
Farm Animals (set/8)
Issued: 1995 • Current

#56592
(7)
"Fresh Paint"
New England Village Sign
Issued: 1995 • Current

#56591
(8)
Harvest Pumpkin Wagon
Issued: 1995 • Current

#5645-6
(9)
Harvest Seed Cart (set/3)
Issued: 1992 • Retired: 1995

	ACCESSORIES NEW ENGLAND VILLAGE	Original Price	Status	Market Value	Year Purch.	Price Paid	Value of My Collection
1.	Blue Star Ice Harvesters (set/2)	$27.50	Current	$27.50			
2.	Christmas Bazaar . . . Handmade Quilts (set/2)	$25.00	Current	$25.00			
3.	Christmas Bazaar . . . Woolens & Preserves (set/2)	$25.00	Current	$25.00			
4.	Covered Wooden Bridge	$10.00	Retired	$43.00			
5.	Farm Animals (set/4)	$15.00	Retired	$46.00			
6.	Farm Animals (set/8)	$32.50	Current	$32.50			
7.	"Fresh Paint" New England Village Sign	$20.00	Current	$20.00			

8.	Harvest Pumpkin Wagon
	• Variation: "Horse-Drawn
	  Squash Cart" - Bachman's
	  Exclusive, 110th Anniversary
		$45.00
		
		$50.00
			Current
			
			Retired
				$45.00
				
				$110.00			

9.	Harvest Seed Cart (set/3)	$27.50	Retired	$43.00			

✏️ **PENCIL TOTALS**

	PRICE PAID	MARKET VALUE

#5649-9 ① **Knife Grinder (set/2)** Issued: 1993 • Retired: 1996	**#56589** ② **Lobster Trappers (set/4)** Issued: 1995 • Current	**#56590** ③ **Lumberjacks (set/2)** Issued: 1995 • Current
#6589-7 ④ **Maple Sugaring Shed (set/3)** Issued: 1987 • Retired: 1989	**#5641-3** ⑤ **Market Day (set/3)** Issued: 1991 • Retired: 1993	**#6570-6** ⑥ **New England Village Sign** Issued: 1987 • Retired: 1993
#6532-3 ⑦ **New England Winter Set (set/5)** Issued: 1986 • Retired: 1990	**#56593** ⑧ **NEW!** **A New Potbellied Stove For Christmas (set/2)** Issued: 1996 • Current	**#5655-3** ⑨ **The Old Man And The Sea (set/3)** Issued: 1994 • Current

ACCESSORIES – NEW ENGLAND VILLAGE (side tab)

	ACCESSORIES NEW ENGLAND VILLAGE	Original Price	Status	Market Value	Year Purch.	Price Paid	Value of My Collection
1.	Knife Grinder (set/2)	$22.50	Retired	$26.00			
2.	Lobster Trappers (set/4)	$35.00	Current	$35.00			
3.	Lumberjacks (set/2)	$30.00	Current	$30.00			
4.	Maple Sugaring Shed (set/3)	$19.00	Retired	$242.00			
5.	Market Day (set/3)	$35.00	Retired	$57.00			
6.	New England Village Sign	$6.00	Retired	$20.00			
7.	New England Winter Set (set/5)	$18.00	Retired	$52.00			
8.	A New Potbellied Stove For Christmas (set/2)	$35.00	Current	$35.00			
9.	The Old Man And The Sea (set/3)	$25.00	Current	$25.00			
	✏ PENCIL TOTALS					PRICE PAID	MARKET VALUE

1 #5654-5

Over The River And Through The Woods
Issued: 1994 • Current

2 #5987-0

Red Covered Bridge
Issued: 1988 • Retired: 1994

3 #5956-0

Sleepy Hollow Characters (set/3)
Issued: 1990 • Retired: 1992

4 #6511-0

Sleighride
Issued: 1986 • Retired: 1990

5 #5646-4

Town Tinker (set/2)
Issued: 1992 • Retired: 1995

6 #5941-2

Village Harvest People (set/4)
Issued: 1988 • Retired: 1991

7 #5986-2

Woodcutter & Son (set/2)
Issued: 1988 • Retired: 1990

8 #56182

**"Alpen Horn Player"
Alpine Village Sign**
Issued: 1995 • Current

9 #6571-4

Alpine Village Sign
Issued: 1987 • Retired: 1993

	ACCESSORIES NEW ENGLAND VILLAGE	Original Price	Status	Market Value	Year Purch.	Price Paid	Value of My Collection
1.	Over The River And Through The Woods	$35.00	Current	$35.00			
2.	Red Covered Bridge	$15.00	Retired	$30.00			
3.	Sleepy Hollow Characters (set/3)	$27.50	Retired	$48.00			
4.	Sleighride	$19.50	Retired	$57.00			
5.	Town Tinker (set/2)	$24.00	Retired	$32.00			
6.	Village Harvest People (set/4)	$27.50	Retired	$53.00			
7.	Woodcutter & Son (set/2)	$10.00	Retired	$55.00			
	ACCESSORIES ALPINE VILLAGE						
8.	"Alpen Horn Player" Alpine Village Sign	$20.00	Current	$20.00			
9.	Alpine Village Sign	$6.00	Retired	$20.00			
				✎ PENCIL TOTALS			
						Price Paid	Market Value

| # | #6542-0 | #5619-7 | #5613-8 |

1 #6542-0
Alpine Villagers (set/3)
Issued: 1986 • Retired: 1992

2 #5619-7
Buying Bakers Bread (set/2)
Issued: 1992 • Retired: 1995

3 #5613-8
Climb Every Mountain (set/4)
Issued: 1993 • Current

4 NEW! #56183
Nutcracker Vendor & Cart
Issued: 1996 • Current

5 #5607-3
Polka Fest (set/3)
Issued: 1994 • Current

6 #56180
"Silent Night" Music Box
Issued: 1995 • Current

7 #5616-2
The Toy Peddler (set/3)
Issued: 1990 • Current

8 #5545-0
All Around The Town (set/2)
Issued: 1991 • Retired: 1993

9 #5964-1
Automobiles (set/3)
Issued: 1987 • Retired: 1996

ACCESSORIES
ALPINE/CHRISTMAS

ACCESSORIES ALPINE VILLAGE	Original Price	Status	Market Value	Year Purch.	Price Paid	Value of My Collection
1. Alpine Villagers (set/3)	$13.00	Retired	$36.00			
2. Buying Bakers Bread (set/2)	$20.00	Retired	$25.00			
3. Climb Every Mountain (set/4)	$27.50	Current	$27.50			
4. Nutcracker Vendor & Cart	$25.00	Current	$25.00			
5. Polka Fest (set/3)	$30.00	Current	$30.00			
6. "Silent Night" Music Box	$32.50	Current	$32.50			
7. The Toy Peddler (set/3)	$22.00	Current	$22.00			
ACCESSORIES CHRISTMAS IN THE CITY						
8. All Around The Town (set/2)	$18.00	Retired	$34.00			
9. Automobiles (set/3)	$15.00	Retired	$28.00			
✎ PENCIL TOTALS					PRICE PAID	MARKET VALUE

1	#5516-6	2	#5535-2	3	#5548-4

Boulevard (set/14)
Issued: 1989 • Retired: 1992

Busy Sidewalks (set/4)
Issued: 1990 • Retired: 1992

Caroling Thru The City (set/3)
Issued: 1991 • Current

Central Park Carriage
Issued: 1989 • Current

Chamber Orchestra (set/4)
Issued: 1994 • Current

Choirboys All-In-A-Row
Issued: 1995 • Current

Christmas In The City Sign
Issued: 1987 • Retired: 1993

City Bus & Milk Truck (set/2)
Issued: 1988 • Retired: 1991

"City Fire Dept.", Fire Truck (set/3)
Issued: 1991 • Retired: 1995

	ACCESSORIES CHRISTMAS IN THE CITY	Original Price	Status	Market Value	Year Purch.	Price Paid	Value of My Collection
1.	Boulevard (set/14)	$25.00	Retired	$58.00			
2.	Busy Sidewalks (set/4)	$28.00	Retired	$48.00			
3.	Caroling Thru The City (set/3)	$27.50	Current	$27.50			
4.	Central Park Carriage	$30.00	Current	$30.00			
5.	Chamber Orchestra (set/4)	$35.00	Current	$37.50			
6.	Choirboys All-In-A-Row	$20.00	Current	$20.00			
7.	Christmas In The City Sign	$6.00	Retired	$20.00			
8.	City Bus & Milk Truck (set/2)	$15.00	Retired	$37.00			
9.	"City Fire Dept.", Fire Truck (set/3)	$18.00	Retired	$30.00			
		PENCIL TOTALS				PRICE PAID	MARKET VALUE

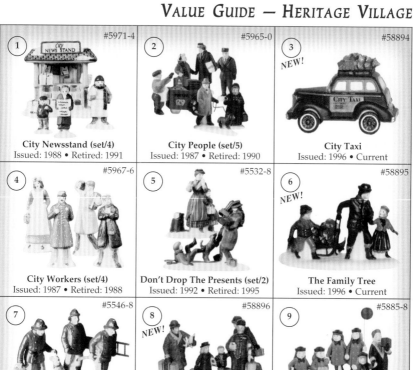

#			
1 #5971-4	**2** #5965-0	**3** NEW! #58894	

City Newsstand (set/4)
Issued: 1988 • Retired: 1991

City People (set/5)
Issued: 1987 • Retired: 1990

City Taxi
Issued: 1996 • Current

4 #5967-6 · **5** #5532-8 · **6** NEW! #58895

City Workers (set/4)
Issued: 1987 • Retired: 1988

Don't Drop The Presents (set/2)
Issued: 1992 • Retired: 1995

The Family Tree
Issued: 1996 • Current

7 #5546-8 · **8** NEW! #58896 · **9** #5885-8

The Fire Brigade (set/2)
Issued: 1991 • Retired: 1995

Going Home For The Holidays (set/3)
Issued: 1996 • Current

Holiday Field Trip (set/3)
Issued: 1994 • Current

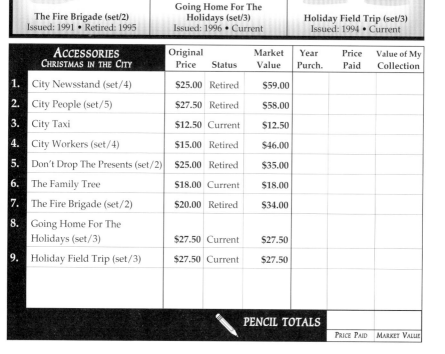

	ACCESSORIES CHRISTMAS IN THE CITY	Original Price	Status	Market Value	Year Purch.	Price Paid	Value of My Collection
1.	City Newsstand (set/4)	$25.00	Retired	$59.00			
2.	City People (set/5)	$27.50	Retired	$58.00			
3.	City Taxi	$12.50	Current	$12.50			
4.	City Workers (set/4)	$15.00	Retired	$46.00			
5.	Don't Drop The Presents (set/2)	$25.00	Retired	$35.00			
6.	The Family Tree	$18.00	Current	$18.00			
7.	The Fire Brigade (set/2)	$20.00	Retired	$34.00			
8.	Going Home For The Holidays (set/3)	$27.50	Current	$27.50			
9.	Holiday Field Trip (set/3)	$27.50	Current	$27.50			

✏️ **PENCIL TOTALS**

	PRICE PAID	MARKET VALUE

ACCESSORIES CHRISTMAS IN THE CITY

1	#5886-6	Hot Dog Vendor (set/3) Issued: 1994 • Current
2	#58893	"A Key To The City" Christmas In The City Sign Issued: 1995 • Current
3	#5517-4	Mailbox & Fire Hydrant (set/2, red, white & blue) Issued: 1989 • Retired: 1990
4	#5214-0	Mailbox & Fire Hydrant (set/2, green & red) Issued: 1990 • Current
5	#58891	One-Man Band And The Dancing Dog (set/2) Issued: 1995 • Current
6	#5957-9	Organ Grinder (set/3) Issued: 1989 • Retired: 1991
7	#5958-7	Popcorn Vendor (set/3) Issued: 1989 • Retired: 1992
8	#5540-9	Rest Ye Merry Gentlemen Issued: 1990 • Current
9	#5959-5	River Street Ice House Cart Issued: 1989 • Retired: 1991

	ACCESSORIES CHRISTMAS IN THE CITY	Original Price	Status	Market Value	Year Purch.	Price Paid	Value of My Collection
1.	Hot Dog Vendor (set/3)	$27.50	Current	$27.50			
2.	"A Key To The City" Christmas In The City Sign	$20.00	Current	$20.00			
3.	Mailbox & Fire Hydrant (set/2, red, white & blue)	$6.00	Retired	$24.00			
4.	Mailbox & Fire Hydrant (set/2, green & red)	$5.00	Current	$5.00			
5.	One-Man Band And The Dancing Dog (set/2)	$17.50	Current	$17.50			
6.	Organ Grinder (set/3)	$21.00	Retired	$43.00			
7.	Popcorn Vendor (set/3)	$22.00	Retired	$37.00			
8.	Rest Ye Merry Gentlemen	$12.50	Current	$12.95			
9.	River Street Ice House Cart	$20.00	Retired	$53.00			

PENCIL TOTALS

PRICE PAID	MARKET VALUE

#5985-4 (1)
Salvation Army Band (set/6)
Issued: 1988 • Retired: 1991

#5564-6 (2)
Street Musicians (set/3)
Issued: 1993 • Current

#5539-5 (3)
'Tis The Season
Issued: 1990 • Retired: 1994

#5533-6 (4)
Welcome Home (set/3)
Issued: 1992 • Retired: 1995

#58890 (5)
"Yes, Virginia . . ." (set/2)
Issued: 1995 • Current

#5603-0 (6)
Baker Elves (set/3)
Issued: 1991 • Retired: 1995

#56366 (7)
"A Busy Elf" North Pole Sign
Issued: 1995 • Current

#52621 (8)
Candy Cane Lampposts (set/4)
Issued: 1996 • Current

#56364 (9)
Charting Santa's Course (set/2)
Issued: 1995 • Current

ACCESSORIES
CHRISTMAS/NORTH POLE

	ACCESSORIES CHRISTMAS IN THE CITY	Original Price	Status	Market Value	Year Purch.	Price Paid	Value of My Collection
1.	Salvation Army Band (set/6)	$24.00	Retired	$82.00			
2.	Street Musicians (set/3)	$25.00	Current	$25.00			
3.	'Tis The Season	$12.50	Retired	$26.00		.	
4.	Welcome Home (set/3)	$27.50	Retired	$36.00			
5.	"Yes, Virginia..." (set/2)	$12.50	Current	$12.50			
	ACCESSORIES NORTH POLE						
6.	Baker Elves (set/3)	$27.50	Retired	$49.00			
7.	"A Busy Elf" North Pole Sign	$20.00	Current	$20.00			
8.	Candy Cane Lampposts (set/4)	$13.00	Current	$13.00			
9.	Charting Santa's Course (set/2)	$25.00	Current	$25.00			

✎ **PENCIL TOTALS**

PRICE PAID	MARKET VALUE

1 NEW! #56369
Early Rising Elves (set/5)
Issued: 1996 • Current

2 #52298
Elves On Ice (set/4)
Issued: 1996 • Current

3 NEW! #56370
End Of The Line (set/2)
Issued: 1996 • Current

4 NEW! #56371
Holiday Deliveries
Issued: 1996 • Current

5 #56365
I'll Need More Toys (set/2)
Issued: 1995 • Current

6 #5636-7
Last Minute Delivery
Issued: 1994 • Current

7 #5604-9
Letters For Santa (set/3)
Issued: 1992 • Retired: 1994

8 NEW! #56368
North Pole Express
Issued: 1996 • Current

9 #5632-4
North Pole Gate
Issued: 1993 • Current

	ACCESSORIES NORTH POLE	Original Price	Status	Market Value	Year Purch.	Price Paid	Value of My Collection
1.	Early Rising Elves (set/5)	$32.50	Current	$32.50			
2.	Elves On Ice (set/4)	$7.50	Current	$7.50			
3.	End Of The Line (set/2)	$28.00	Current	$28.00			
4.	Holiday Deliveries	$16.50	Current	$16.50			
5.	I'll Need More Toys (set/2)	$25.00	Current	$25.00			
6.	Last Minute Delivery	$35.00	Current	$35.00			
7.	Letters For Santa (set/3)	$30.00	Retired	$58.00			
8.	North Pole Express	$37.50	Current	$37.50			
9.	North Pole Gate	$32.50	Current	$32.50			
	PENCIL TOTALS					PRICE PAID	MARKET VALUE

#5609-0
1 — Santa & Mrs. Claus (set/2)
Issued: 1990 • Current

#5610-3
2 — Santa's Little Helpers (set/3)
Issued: 1990 • Retired: 1993

#5631-6
3 — Sing A Song For Santa (set/3)
Issued: 1993 • Current

#5611-1
4 — Sleigh & Eight Tiny Reindeer (set/5)
Issued: 1990 • Current

#5637-5
5 — Snow Cone Elves (set/4)
Issued: 1994 • Current

#5605-7
6 — Testing The Toys (set/2)
Issued: 1992 • Current

#5602-2
7 — Toymaker Elves (set/3)
Issued: 1991 • Retired: 1995

#5608-1
8 — Trimming The North Pole
Issued: 1990 • Retired: 1993

#5630-8
9 — Woodsmen Elves (set/3)
Issued: 1993 • Retired: 1995

ACCESSORIES
NORTH POLE

	ACCESSORIES NORTH POLE	Original Price	Status	Market Value	Year Purch.	Price Paid	Value of My Collection
1.	Santa & Mrs. Claus (set/2)	$15.00	Current	$15.00			
2.	Santa's Little Helpers (set/3)	$28.00	Retired	$56.00			
3.	Sing A Song For Santa (set/3)	$28.00	Current	$28.00			
4.	Sleigh & Eight Tiny Reindeer (set/5)	$40.00	Current	$42.00			
5.	Snow Cone Elves (set/4)	$30.00	Current	$30.00			
6.	Testing The Toys (set/2)	$16.50	Current	$16.50			
7.	Toymaker Elves (set/3)	$27.50	Retired	$44.00			
8.	Trimming The North Pole	$10.00	Retired	$30.00			
9.	Woodsmen Elves (set/3)	$30.00	Retired	$52.00			
	PENCIL TOTALS					PRICE PAID	MARKET VALUE

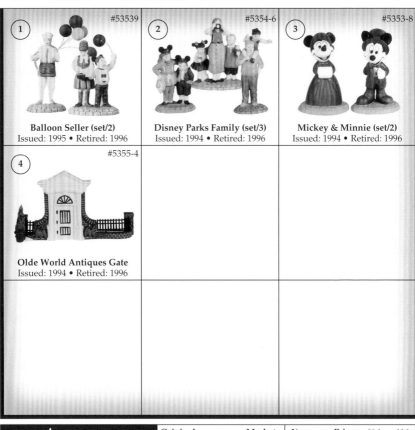

#53539

(1)

Balloon Seller (set/2)
Issued: 1995 • Retired: 1996

#5354-6

(2)

Disney Parks Family (set/3)
Issued: 1994 • Retired: 1996

#5353-8

(3)

Mickey & Minnie (set/2)
Issued: 1994 • Retired: 1996

#5355-4

(4)

Olde World Antiques Gate
Issued: 1994 • Retired: 1996

	ACCESSORIES DISNEY PARKS VILLAGE SERIES	Original Price	Status	Market Value	Year Purch.	Price Paid	Value of My Collection
1.	Balloon Seller (set/2)	$25.00	Retired	$44.00			
2.	Disney Parks Family (set/3)	$32.50	Retired	$40.00			
3.	Mickey & Minnie (set/2)	$22.50	Retired	$29.00			
4.	Olde World Antiques Gate	$15.00	Retired	$18.00			

✎ **PENCIL TOTALS**

|3|

PRICE PAID	MARKET VALUE

Use this page to record future Heritage Village accessories.

ACCESSORIES HERITAGE VILLAGE	Original Price	Status	Market Value	Year Purch.	Price Paid	Value of My Collection
				PENCIL TOTALS	Price Paid	Market Value

Total Value Of My Collection

*Record the value of your collection here by adding the pencil totals
from the bottom of each value guide page.*

DICKENS' VILLAGE

	Price Paid	Market Value
Page 31		
Page 32		
Page 33		
Page 34		
Page 35		
Page 36		
Page 37		
Page 38		
Page 39		
Page 40		
Page 41		
Page 42		
Page 43		
Page 60		
TOTAL		

NEW ENGLAND VILLAGE

	Price Paid	Market Value
Page 43		
Page 44		
Page 45		
Page 46		
Page 47		
Page 48		
Page 60		
TOTAL		

ALPINE VILLAGE

	Price Paid	Market Value
Page 48		
Page 49		
Page 50		
Page 60		
TOTAL		

CHRISTMAS IN THE CITY

	Price Paid	Market Value
Page 50		
Page 51		
Page 52		
Page 53		
Page 54		
Page 60		
TOTAL		

NORTH POLE

	Price Paid	Market Value
Page 55		
Page 56		
Page 57		
Page 58		
Page 60		
TOTAL		

DISNEY PARKS VILLAGE SERIES

	Price Paid	Market Value
Page 59		
TOTAL		

LITTLE TOWN OF BETHLEHEM

	Price Paid	Market Value
Page 59		
TOTAL		

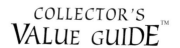

COLLECTOR'S
VALUE GUIDE™

Total Value Of My Collection

ACCESSORIES GENERAL HERITAGE VILLAGE	Price Paid	Market Value
Page 61		
Page 62		
Page 63		
Page 64		
Page 85		
TOTAL		

ACCESSORIES DICKENS' VILLAGE	Price Paid	Market Value
Page 65		
Page 66		
Page 67		
Page 68		
Page 69		
Page 70		
Page 71		
Page 72		
Page 73		
Page 85		
TOTAL		

ACCESSORIES NEW ENGLAND VILLAGE	Price Paid	Market Value
Page 73		
Page 74		
Page 75		
Page 76		
Page 85		
TOTAL		

ACCESSORIES ALPINE VILLAGE	Price Paid	Market Value
Page 76		
Page 77		
Page 85		
TOTAL		

ACCESSORIES CHRISTMAS IN THE CITY	Price Paid	Market Value
Page 77		
Page 78		
Page 79		
Page 80		
Page 81		
Page 85		
TOTAL		

ACCESSORIES NORTH POLE	Price Paid	Market Value
Page 81		
Page 82		
Page 83		
Page 85		
TOTAL		

ACCESSORIES DISNEY PARKS VILLAGE SERIES	Price Paid	Market Value
Page 84		
TOTAL		

GRAND TOTALS	PRICE PAID	MARKET VALUE

COLLECTOR'S
VALUE GUIDE™

Snow Village Overview

The Original Snow Village

The Original Snow Village debuted in 1976 with six rough-looking, colorful lighted buildings. From these humble beginnings, Snow Village has grown to include 199 releases and 140 accessories. Since the first year of the collection, Snow Village collectors have witnessed the evolution of a small community of cottages and churches into a bustling, vibrant society. A recent trend in Snow Village is the addition of recognizable brand names and actual landmarks, like "Coca Cola® Brand Bottling Plant" (1994), "Starbucks Coffee" (1995) and the famous "Ryman Auditorium" (1995), home of the Grand Ole Opry. And now this quiet little village will never be quite the same as the "Harley-Davidson Motorcycle Shop" roars into town and sets up shop in 1997.

The buildings in The Original Snow Village are reminiscent of small American towns from the 1930s to the 1960s, and include pieces like "The Honeymooner Motel" with its 25-cent soda machine and the "Paramount Theater" with the movie "White Christmas" on the marquee and a sign promising that "It's A Wonderful Life" is *coming soon!* The 1950s lives on in the new "Rockabilly Records," while the new "Christmas Lake High School" perpetuates the poodle skirt by advertising a "sock hop." Snow Village accessories also add to the sense of nostalgia, particularly with vehicles such as the wood-paneled "Woody Station Wagon" (1988), the finned police car in "Calling All Cars" (1989) and the pink "Christmas Cadillac" (1991).

While private homes and churches made up the majority of early Snow Village releases, it didn't take long for the first small-town business to establish themselves. Snow Village first became "commercialized" in 1978, with the introduction of the "General Store." The "General Store" maintained its monopoly until the introduction of the "Corner Store" and the "Bakery" in 1981. From the early 1980s and on through the 1990s, the Original Snow Village has undergone a commercial boom, with introductions such as the "Bank" (1982), "Grocery" (1983), "Apothecary" (1986), "Service Station" (1988), "Al's TV Shop" (1992) and "Dinah's Drive-In" (1993), to just name of few. The latest

COLLECTOR'S
VALUE GUIDE™

Snow Village Overview

new shops to open in Snow Village include "The Secret Garden Florist" and a new Mexican restaurant, "Rosita's Cantina." As the village has grown, the villagers have found new and sometimes creative modes of transportation. In addition to train stations, an airport, taxi cabs and school buses, several recent car accessories and the new "Harley-Davidson Fat Boy & Softail" help Snow Villagers get around town. With more and more cars traveling Snow Village roads, the new "Terry's Towing" (set/2) and "Men At Work" (set/5) will be an important part of village life.

Unlike its Heritage Village counterpart, there are no true sub-collections within The Original Snow Village. However, in 1990, an informal series was introduced called the *American Architecture Series*, which debuted with "Prairie House" and "Queen Anne Victorian." This series celebrates traditional American homes and depicts a variety of architectural styles. In the following seven years, the series has grown to eight pieces, including this year's "Shingle Victorian."

As Snow Village grows, it is inevitable that pieces must be retired in order to make room for exciting new releases. Snow Village retirements are announced annually by Department 56 (in 1996, the retirements were unveiled in November). The first retirements occurred in 1979, three years after the introduction of the collection and included the original six pieces. The announcement of such retirements has become an eagerly-anticipated event for some collectors because they generally boost the value of the Snow Village pieces on the secondary market as they become less readily available.

What's New In Snow Village

This section highlights the new Snow Village releases for 1997. This year features 8 new buildings and 11 new accessories.

Birch Run Ski Chalet . . . The whole village is buzzing about the new ski chalet which offers all the amenities of a cozy winter haven for skiers to warm themselves between runs down the slopes. To the right is a station offering beginner ski lessons and a first aid station for those who didn't pay attention during their lessons. A log cabin structure with a built-in fireplace, this winter chalet provides a rustic atmosphere in which skiers can relax after a hard day at play. Racks attached to the front of the building provide a storage place for skis while patrons enjoy the full-service restaurant where there's a special on hot chocolate all day long!

Birch Run Ski Chalet
- #54882
Snow Village

Christmas Lake High School . . . As the school bell chimes from a tower fixed in the center of a steepled blue roof, students scurry up the steps to avoid being late for their first class. The American flag proudly waves underneath a sign marking the school's first year, "1909," while a sign on the side of the building advertises the class of 1956's sock hop. The name of this piece is never more fitting as it is during this time of year; all decorated with wreaths and spotted with snow, the school rings with holiday cheer!

Christmas Lake High
School - #54881
Snow Village

Harley-Davidson Motorcycle Shop . . . This year, Harley-Davidson rides into town with a selection of new and used bikes. The classic Harley-Davidson Motorcycle sign sits atop the store as one of the current year's models is proudly displayed on a ledge above the entrance. The garage to the right is open for service and the gas pump in front is used to fill up empty "hogs." While you're satisfying your gas tank's thirst, you can quench your own with an ice cold soda pop from the cooler - the perfect break from a long ride!

Harley-Davidson Motorcycle
Shop - 54886
Snow Village

COLLECTOR'S
VALUE GUIDE™

What's New In Snow Village

***Rockabilly Records* . . .** "One, two, three o'clock, four o'clock rock" is just one rocking example of what serenades the patrons of "Rockabilly Records" as they browse throught the stacks in search of their favorite 45s. At any given time (and depending on the mood of the on-duty clerk, who might be caught tapping his foot or whistling along with his favorite tune), classical, jazz, country, as well as scores of other types of music, can be heard on the many record players throughout the shop. Outside, music notes dance across an album, singing the store's name from the top of the building, while jukeboxes on each side of the store play music upon request (for the small fee of a dime).

Rockabilly Records
- #54880
Snow Village

***Rosita's Cantina* . . .** Take off your sombrero, kick up your heels and get ready to enjoy a most authentic mexican meal! "Rosita's Cantina" is *the hot spot* for both tourists and townies within Snow Village. Everything about Rosita's says "Mexican" from the southwestern stucco design to the colorful decor and cactus plants surrounding the front landing. Collectors are sure to enjoy a festive fiesta when they add this piece to their collections.

Rosita's Cantina - #54883
Snow Village

***The Secret Garden Florist* . . .** Collectors will be sure to wake up and smell the roses when this piece is added to their collection. Under an awning displaying the store's name, beautiful bouquets have been greeting patrons who have come to rely on the floral expertise of the shop since 1936. A plaque hangs from the second story level advertising that weddings are their forté with a full-time planner available to assist with all the arrangements for the special day. Whatever the occasion may be, "The Secret Garden Florist" is ready to make it special!

The Secret Garden
Florist - #54885
Snow Village

COLLECTOR'S
VALUE GUIDE™

What's New In Snow Village

Shingle Victorian . . . The eighth piece in the *American Architecture Series,* "Shingle Victorian," is characteristic of the Victorian-style homes prevalent during the early 1900s. A wood deck extends from the front doors and wraps around the right side of this historical home. Alcove windows jut from a snow-spotted roof and it's not difficult to imagine smoke pouring out of its dual chimneys. The lower level of the house is made of white wood while the upper level is embellished with light blue shingles and accented with darker blue shutters and trimming. Lovely Christmas wreaths adorn all of the windows while dark gray tile covers a steeple-shaped rooftop and adds a nice finishing touch to this beautiful home, which any village family would be proud to call their own!

Shingle Victorian (*American Architecture Series*) - #54884
Snow Village

Treetop Tree House . . . Tucked away in a giant spruce tree, the "Treetop Tree House" is the perfect hide-a-way playhouse for all the young Snow Villagers. Nestled between sturdy branches and ever-slightly slanted, the treehouse is perched on a wooden plank base and constructed of logs and sticks (a testimonial to the age of its architects). Throughout all four seasons, laughter can be heard flowing from the house for miles! A "club" sign on the door emphasizes this establishment was made for members only, but the buzz around the village is that the club isn't all that exclusive. In fact, anyone willing to brave climbing up the red ladder is more than welcome to join. And the qualifications for becoming club president are quite simple too – the little villager who can swing the highest on the tire swing is the one most worthy of the office!

Treetop Tree House
- #54890
Snow Village

What's New In Snow Village

Snow Village Accessories . . . Harley-Davidson appears as a major theme of the season, from the shining chrome of twin motorcycles, "Harley-Davidson Fat Boy & Softail," to the sidecar packed with presents in "A Harley-Davidson Holiday" (set/2). The "Harley-Davidson Sign" meant to complement the "Harley-Davidson Motorcycle Shop" proudly displays the slogan, "Live To Ride, Ride To Live," suggesting that riding a "hog" is a lifestyle and not just a mode of transportation.

With so much to do before Christmas, the villagers find that they have a greater need for mobility and this year Department 56 introduces several new cars to Snow Village. In "Heading For The Hills" (2 asst.), the skis are strapped to the racks on top, the trunks are full of boots, hats and gloves and the vanity license plates ("2 Ski") leave no doubt as to where these cars are headed. The travel theme carries on with "On the Road Again" (set/2) as a station wagon with camper in tow and canoe strapped to the top makes its way towards its holiday destination.

For those whose holiday travel is a bit more permanent, there's "Moving Day" (set/3). The Holiday Movers moving company makes moving easy and stress-free with the promise "We'll make your moving day feel like a holiday," printed boldly on the side of their van. It looks like this family can use the help as a teddy bear sits upon an upside-down box and the family dog expresses his reluctance to leave his old home.

Harley-Davidson Fat Boy
& Softail - #54900
Snow Village

A Harley-Davidson
Holiday (set/2) - #54898
Snow Village

Harley-Davidson Sign
- #54901
Snow Village

Heading For The Hills
(2 asst.) - #54897
Snow Village

On The Road Again
(set/2) - #54891
Snow Village

Moving Day (set/3)
- #54892
Snow Village

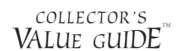

COLLECTOR'S
VALUE GUIDE™

What's New In Snow Village

If holiday travelers have a problem on the road, they can rely on "Terry's Towing" (set/2) to come to the rescue. The easy-to-remember phone number "555-TOW-U" (the license plate also spells out "TOW-U") is painted right on the side of the truck for all to see. But as with any winter season, there's plenty of business for Terry which is evident with the car that he has in tow. And while Terry works to fix problems, the road crews of "Men At Work" (set/5) are hard at work repairing winter damage. A bulldozer waits behind three workers as one directs traffic, one diligently shovels and the third works with a jackhammer. Signs caution motorists of road work ahead and to stop for oncoming traffic.

Don't let it be said that all work and no play makes a dull Snow Villager as these new accessories depict the townies doing what they do best – having fun! In a sleigh guided by a favorite teddy bear and pushed along by an older brother, two young carolers serenade villagers throughout the town square with songs of holiday joy in "Caroling Through The Snow." And in "Holiday Hoops" (set/3), two young boys test out their jump shots in a friendly game of winter basketball.

And at the end of the day, the Snow Villagers snuggle into their beds and fall asleep with visions of sugarplums dancing in their heads as "Santa Comes To Town, 1997." This limited edition piece is the third in an annual series.

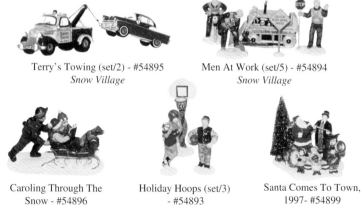

Terry's Towing (set/2) - #54895
Snow Village

Men At Work (set/5) - #54894
Snow Village

Caroling Through The
Snow - #54896
Snow Village

Holiday Hoops (set/3)
- #54893
Snow Village

Santa Comes To Town,
1997- #54899
Snow Village

COLLECTOR'S
VALUE GUIDE™

What's New In Snow Village

Recent Retirements

Department 56 announces new retirements for Snow Village each year and for the past several years the list has been published in *USA Today*. The following pieces (listed with issue year in parentheses) were retired on November 8, 1996.

The Original Snow Village

- ❏ Airport (1992)
- ❏ The Christmas Shop (1991)
- ❏ Dinah's Drive-In (1993)
- ❏ Dutch Colonial (1995, *American Architecture Seres*)
- ❏ Good Shepherd Chapel & Church School (1992, set/2)
- ❏ Grandma's Cottage (1992)
- ❏ Hunting Lodge (1993)
- ❏ Mount Olivet Church (1993)
- ❏ The Original Snow Village Starter Set (1994, set/6)
- ❏ *Shady Oak Church*
- ❏ *Sunday School Serenade (accessory)*
- ❏ Queen Anne Victorian (1990, *American Architecture Series*)
- ❏ Snowy Hills Hospital (1993)
- ❏ Woodbury House (1993)

The Original Snow Village Accessories

- ❏ Christmas At The Farm (1993, set/2)
- ❏ Christmas Puppies (1992, set/2)
- ❏ Crack The Whip (1989, set/3)
- ❏ A Home For The Holidays (1990)
- ❏ Pint-Size Pony Rides (1993, set/3)
- ❏ Santa Comes To Town, 1996 (1995)
- ❏ Spirit Of Snow Village Airplane (1992)
- ❏ Spirit Of Snow Village Airplane (1993, 2 assorted)
- ❏ Village News Delivery (1993, set/2)

COLLECTOR'S
VALUE GUIDE™

Snow Village Top Ten

Top Ten Most Valuable Snow Village Pieces

This section highlights the ten most valuable Snow Village pieces as determined by demand on the secondary market. To qualify for the top ten, pieces have to have top dollar value and show a significant percentage of increase in value from their original prices (as shown by our market meter). Many pieces in the Top Ten had short production runs or tended to have lower quantities available because the subject matter attracted buyers from outside of Department 56 collector circles.

#1 CATHEDRAL CHURCH (1980)

#5067-4
Issued 1980 — Retired 1981
Issue Price: $36
Secondary Market Price: $2,540
Market Meter: +6,956%

One of five churches in the Top Ten, "Cathedral Church" has earned its #1 ranking for a variety of reasons. Churches are a consistent favorite with Snow Village collectors, and this majestic piece towers over its peers. Because of a complex design which caused many production problems, including the collapse of the dome during the firing process, the "Cathedral Church" was produced for only one year. The one year production coupled with the existence of numerous damaged pieces have helped make this church very rare on the secondary market. Another "Cathedral Church" (#5019-9) was issued in 1987 with a completely different design.

COLLECTOR'S
VALUE GUIDE™

96

#2 ADOBE HOUSE

#5066-6
Issued 1979 — Retired 1980
Issue Price: $18
Secondary Market Price: $2,520
Market Meter: +13,900%

The story of Snow Village's "Adobe House" offers what is perhaps one of the best lessons for collectors who are interested in the eventual secondary market value of their collections: good looks *do not* necessarily equal good value. The "Adobe House" is distinctive as it is one of the few pieces in Snow Village with a genuine Southwestern flair. Still, it did not catch on with collectors and it was retired after only one year of production. The end result: a secondary market explosion! "Adobe House" is one of only two retired Snow Village buildings currently valued at over $2,000. Quite an achievement for an "undesirable" piece that was issued for only $18!

#3 MOBILE HOME

#5063-3
Issued 1979 — Retired 1980
Issue Price: $18
Secondary Market Price: $1,990
Market Meter: +10,955%

Not very popular with collectors when it was first issued, the "Mobile Home" had greater appeal to mobile home enthusiasts who took pride in the silver Airstream-style design. In the early years of Snow Village, displays weren't as sophisticated as many have become today and collectors may not have envisioned a campground for mobile homes in a secluded area of their display. The "Mobile Home" was only available for one year and the limited supply has made this "home on wheels" one of the most sought after pieces in the collection today.

#4 MISSION CHURCH

#5062-5
Issued 1979 — Retired 1980
Issue Price: $30
Secondary Market Price: $1,240
Market Meter: +4,033%

Like the "Adobe House" (the #2 piece on our top ten list), the Southwestern design of the 1979 issue "Mission Church" was not well-received by collectors and it was retired after only one year of production. Because of the limited quantity and the popularity of churches (some consider the churches a sub-collection within Snow Village), the "Mission Church" has become one of the most coveted Snow Village retired designs.

#5 SKATING RINK/ DUCK POND SET

#5015-3
Issued 1978 — Retired 1979
Issue Price: $16
Secondary Market Price: $1,000
Market Meter: +6,150%

The two ponds in the "Skating Rink/Duck Pond Set" were the first non-buildings released. Each piece consists of a small pond surrounded by snowbanks and one large lighted tree. The large, heavy trees were attached to a small, flat base which caused many of the pieces to break and production ceased after only one year. It was another four years before another pond was introduced to the village (with trees attached by a sturdier two-part mold, of course).

#6 STONE CHURCH (1979)

#5059-1
Issued 1979 — Retired 1980
Issue Price: $32
Secondary Market Price: $970
Market Meter: +2,931%

Three stone churches have been issued in The Original Snow Village and this has caused much confusion among collectors. The first two pieces were released in 1977 and 1979 and shared a very similar appearance, with the key differences being the item number, height, color and the number of holes in the front window above the door (see chart). The 1979 version of "Stone Church," pictured above, was available for just one year and is the #6 most valuable piece on our list. The original 1977 version was available for only two years. The 1982 piece is called "New Stone Church" and has a different design than the first two releases.

	1977	1979
Item #	5009-6	5059-1
Height	10.5"	8.5"
Color	pale yellow or light mint green	bright yellow
Window holes	3	6 or more

#7 CONGREGATIONAL CHURCH

#5034-2
Issued 1984 — Retired 1985
Issue Price: $28
Secondary Market Price: $640
Market Meter: +2,186%

Though churches are always popular, this was the first that designated a specific denomination and as such, it attracted casual buyers. Problems with production, a common ingredient among many of the most valuable pieces in this list, forced an early retirement of the "Congregational Church." Through the years, several Department 56 churches have had production difficulties because, as in reality, churches are among the most elaborate and detailed structures in any given community. Pieces with tall and thin extrusions (such as chimney, trees and steeples) have been known to break more easily, both in production and in shipping. The low number of available pieces have driven the price up on the secondary market.

#8 FIRE STATION

#5032-6
Issued 1983 — Retired 1984
Issue Price: $32
Secondary Market Price: $635
Market Meter: +1,884%

The first "Fire Station" in The Original Snow Village is a piece that falls into the "heavy crossover" category. Certain pieces have themes that transcend the "collectibles" consumer base and become popular as gifts. In the one year that this piece was available, it found its way into many firefighters' homes and fire station common areas. Collectors also enjoyed this piece, with its emerging fire truck and delightful Dalmatian, which means that this piece continues to be sought after on the secondary market. A later piece, "Fire Station No. 2" was issued in 1987.

#9 DINER

#5078-4
Issued 1986 — Retired 1987
Issue Price: $22
Secondary Market Price: $630
Market Meter: +2,764%

Known to many collectors simply as "Mickey's," this bright yellow eatery typifies the 1950's-style diner with its railroad car design and gaudy colors. In fact, the piece is supposedly based on a real diner in Minnesota. While this may partially explain its popularity with collectors, the fact that the "Diner" was available for only one year accounts for its rising value on the secondary market. There have been other diners released in Snow Village since the retirement of this colorful piece, but for many collectors, there's just no replacing the original "Diner."

#10 BANK

#5024-5
Issued 1982 — Retired 1983
Issue Price: $32
Secondary Market Price: $610
Market Meter: +1,806%

The "Bank" is another piece that wound up in the homes of many "non-collectors" and because it was only available for one year, it has become a difficult piece to find. It's hard to resist calling this bank a "solid investment" since it has increased in value 1,806% in less than fifteen years!

HONORABLE MENTION:

LIGHTHOUSE

#5030-0
Issued 1987— Retired 1988
Issue Price: $36
Secondary Market Price: $600
Market Meter: +1,567%

The first of only two lighthouses in the collection, "Lighthouse" was available for only one year. Lighthouses are rare and valued pieces to begin with, so it's no surprise that the "Lighthouse" now fetches $600 on the secondary market.

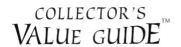

COLLECTOR'S
VALUE GUIDE™

How To Use Your Value Guide

This section lists the entire collection of The Original Snow Village. Lighted buildings are listed first, followed by a separate section of accessories. Every building and accessory is listed alphabetically, making it easy to find your pieces.

How To Total The Value Of Your Collection

The value guide is a great way to keep track of the value of your collection. Simply fill in the blanks for the pieces you own. Put down the year you purchased the piece and the price paid. From the "Market Value" column, find the value and record it in the "Value of My Collection" column.

*Write the **Market Value** of your pieces in the **Value of My Collection** column*

	SNOW VILLAGE	Original Price	Status	Market Value	Year Purch.	Price Paid	Value of My Collection
1.	Corner Cafe	$37.00	Retired	$98.00			
2.	Corner Store	$30.00	Retired	$240.00	1983	30	240
3.	Country Church	$18.00	Retired	$370.00			
4.	Countryside Church	$27.50	Retired	$282.00	1988	40	282
5.	Courthouse	$65.00	Retired	$168.00	1992	65	168
6.	Craftsman Cottage *(American Architecture Series)*	$55.00	Retired	$84.00			
7.	Cumberland House	$42.00	Retired	$75.00			
8.	Dairy Barn	$55.00	Current	$55.00	1996	55	55
9.	Delta House	$32.00	Retired	$300.00	1985	32	300
				PENCIL TOTALS		222 *Price Paid*	1,045 *Market Value*

You can then total the columns at the bottom of the page (use a pencil so you can change totals as your collection grows) and transfer each subtotal to the summary page at the end of the section to come up with the total value of your collection.

#5151-9	#5043-1	#5066-6
1 56 Flavors Ice Cream Parlor Issued: 1990 • Retired: 1992	**2** 2101 Maple Issued: 1986 • Retired: 1986	**3** Adobe House Issued: 1979 • Retired: 1980
#5439-9	#5423-2	#5070-9
4 Airport Issued: 1992 • Retired: 1996	**5** Al's TV Shop Issued: 1992 • Retired: 1995	**6** All Saints Church Issued: 1986 • Current
#5076-8	#5077-6	#5077-6
7 Apothecary Issued: 1986 • Retired: 1990	**8** Bakery Issued: 1981 • Retired: 1983	**9** Bakery Issued: 1986 • Retired: 1991

	SNOW VILLAGE	Original Price	Status	Market Value	Year Purch.	Price Paid	Value of My Collection
1.	56 Flavors Ice Cream Parlor	$42.00	Retired	$113.00			
2.	2101 Maple	$32.00	Retired	$360.00			
3.	Adobe House	$18.00	Retired	$2520.00			
4.	Airport	$60.00	Retired	$72.00			
5.	Al's TV Shop	$40.00	Retired	$63.00			
6.	All Saints Church	$38.00	Current	$45.00			
7.	Apothecary	$34.00	Retired	$108.00			
8.	Bakery (1981)	$30.00	Retired	$267.00			
9.	Bakery (1986)	$35.00	Retired	$90.00			

✏️ PENCIL TOTALS

PRICE PAID	MARKET VALUE

SNOW VILLAGE

1	#5024-5
2	#5074-1
3	#5015-6

Bank
Issued: 1982 • Retired: 1983

Barn
Issued: 1981 • Retired: 1984

Bayport
Issued: 1984 • Retired: 1986

Beacon Hill House
Issued: 1986 • Retired: 1988

Beacon Hill Victorian
Issued: 1995 • Current

Birch Run Ski Chalet
Issued: 1996 • Current

Boulder Springs House
Issued: 1996 • Current

Bowling Alley
Issued: 1995 • Current

Brownstone
Issued: 1979 • Retired: 1981

	SNOW VILLAGE	Original Price	Status	Market Value	Year Purch.	Price Paid	Value of My Collection
1.	Bank	$32.00	Retired	$610.00			
2.	Barn	$32.00	Retired	$454.00			
3.	Bayport	$30.00	Retired	$240.00			
4.	Beacon Hill House	$31.00	Retired	$167.00			
5.	Beacon Hill Victorian	$60.00	Current	$60.00			
6.	Birch Run Ski Chalet	$60.00	Current	$60.00			
7.	Boulder Springs House	$60.00	Current	$60.00			
8.	Bowling Alley	$42.00	Current	$42.00			
9.	Brownstone	$36.00	Retired	$570.00			
					PENCIL TOTALS		
						PRICE PAID	MARKET VALUE

		#5013-8			#5466-6			#5021-0
Cape Cod			Carmel Cottage			Carriage House		
Issued: 1978 • Retired: 1980			Issued: 1994 • Current			Issued: 1982 • Retired: 1984		

		#5071-7			#5067-4			#5019-9
Carriage House			Cathedral Church			Cathedral Church		
Issued: 1986 • Retired: 1988			Issued: 1980 • Retired: 1981			Issued: 1987 • Retired: 1990		

		#5020-2			#5084-9			#5483-6
Centennial House			Chateau			Christmas Cove Lighthouse		
Issued: 1982 • Retired: 1984			Issued: 1983 • Retired: 1984			Issued: 1995 • Current		

	SNOW VILLAGE	Original Price	Status	Market Value	Year Purch.	Price Paid	Value of My Collection
1.	Cape Cod	$20.00	Retired	$394.00			
2.	Carmel Cottage	$48.00	Current	$48.00			
3.	Carriage House (1982, green w/red roof)	$28.00	Retired	$338.00			
4.	Carriage House (1986, white w/black roof)	$29.00	Retired	$120.00			
5.	Cathedral Church (1980)	$36.00	Retired	$2540.00			
6.	Cathedral Church (1987)	$50.00	Retired	$112.00			
7.	Centennial House	$32.00	Retired	$338.00			
8.	Chateau	$35.00	Retired	$465.00			
9.	Christmas Cove Lighthouse	$60.00	Current	$60.00			

✎ PENCIL TOTALS

PRICE PAID	MARKET VALUE

SNOW VILLAGE

#54881	#5097-0	#5048-2
1 NEW!	**2**	**3**
Christmas Lake High School Issued: 1996 • Current	**The Christmas Shop** Issued: 1991 • Retired: 1996	**Church Of The Open Door** Issued: 1985 • Retired: 1988
#5123-3 **4**	#5469-0 **5**	#5484-4 **6**
Cobblestone Antique Shop Issued: 1988 • Retired: 1992	**Coca-Cola® Brand Bottling Plant** Issued: 1994 • Current	**Coca-Cola® Brand Corner Drugstore** Issued: 1995 • Current
#5119-5 **7**	#5070-9 **8**	#5034-2 **9**
Colonial Church Issued: 1989 • Retired: 1992	**Colonial Farm House** Issued: 1980 • Retired: 1982	**Congregational Church** Issued: 1984 • Retired: 1985

	SNOW VILLAGE	Original Price	Status	Market Value	Year Purch.	Price Paid	Value of My Collection
1.	Christmas Lake High School	$52.00	Current	$52.00			
2.	The Christmas Shop	$37.50	Retired	$50.00			
3.	Church Of The Open Door	$34.00	Retired	$140.00			
4.	Cobblestone Antique Shop	$36.00	Retired	$75.00			
5.	Coca Cola® Brand Bottling Plant	$65.00	Current	$65.00			
6.	Coca-Cola® Brand Corner Drugstore	$55.00	Current	$55.00			
7.	Colonial Church	$60.00	Retired	$83.00			
8.	Colonial Farm House	$30.00	Retired	$339.00			
9.	Congregational Church	$28.00	Retired	$640.00			
				✎ PENCIL TOTALS			
						PRICE PAID	MARKET VALUE

1	#5124-1	2	#5076-8	3	#5004-7
Corner Cafe		**Corner Store**		**Country Church**	
Issued: 1988 • Retired: 1991		Issued: 1981 • Retired: 1983		Issued: 1976 • Retired: 1979	

4	#5058-3	5	#5144-6	6	#5437-2
				Craftsman Cottage	
Countryside Church		**Courthouse**		Issued: 1992 • Retired: 1995	
Issued: 1979 • Retired: 1984		Issued: 1989 • Retired: 1993		*American Architecture Series*	

7	#5024-5	8	#5446-1	9	#5012-1
Cumberland House		**Dairy Barn**		**Delta House**	
Issued: 1987 • Retired: 1995		Issued: 1993 • Current		Issued: 1984 • Retired: 1986	

	SNOW VILLAGE	Original Price	Status	Market Value	Year Purch.	Price Paid	Value of My Collection
1.	Corner Cafe	$37.00	Retired	$98.00			
2.	Corner Store	$30.00	Retired	$240.00			
3.	Country Church	$18.00	Retired	$370.00			
4.	Countryside Church	$27.50	Retired	$282.00			
5.	Courthouse	$65.00	Retired	$168.00			
6.	Craftsman Cottage (*American Architecture Series*)	$55.00	Retired	$84.00			
7.	Cumberland House	$42.00	Retired	$75.00			
8.	Dairy Barn	$55.00	Current	$55.00			
9.	Delta House	$32.00	Retired	$300.00			

✎ **PENCIL TOTALS**

PRICE PAID	MARKET VALUE

SNOW VILLAGE

VALUE GUIDE — SNOW VILLAGE

1 #5051-2
**Depot And Train With
2 Train Cars (set/2)**
Issued: 1985 • Retired: 1988

2 #5447-0
Dinah's Drive-In
Issued: 1993 • Retired: 1996

3 #5078-4
Diner
Issued: 1986 • Retired: 1987

4 #5143-8
Doctor's House
Issued: 1989 • Retired: 1992

5 #5407-0
Double Bungalow
Issued: 1991 • Retired: 1994

6 #5050-4
Duplex
Issued: 1985 • Retired: 1987

7 #54856
Dutch Colonial
Issued: 1995 • Retired: 1996
American Architecture Series

8 #5078-4
English Church
Issued: 1981 • Retired: 1982

9 #5073-3
English Cottage
Issued: 1981 • Retired: 1982

	SNOW VILLAGE	Original Price	Status	Market Value	Year Purch.	Price Paid	Value of My Collection
1.	Depot And Train With 2 Train Cars (set/2)	$65.00	Retired	$132.00			
2.	Dinah's Drive-In	$45.00	Retired	$68.00			
3.	Diner	$22.00	Retired	$630.00			
4.	Doctor's House	$56.00	Retired	$107.00			
5.	Double Bungalow	$45.00	Retired	$62.00			
6.	Duplex	$35.00	Retired	$172.00			
7.	Dutch Colonial (*American Architecture Series*)	$45.00	Retired	$60.00			
8.	English Church	$30.00	Retired	$390.00			
9.	English Cottage	$25.00	Retired	$290.00			

✎ **PENCIL TOTALS**

PRICE PAID	MARKET VALUE

#5033-4

English Tudor
Issued: 1983 • Retired: 1985

#5089-0

Farm House
Issued: 1987 • Retired: 1992

#5465-8

Federal House
Issued: 1994 • Current
American Architecture Series

#5405-4

Finklea's Finery: Costume Shop
Issued: 1991 • Retired: 1993

#5032-6

Fire Station
Issued: 1983 • Retired: 1984

#5091-1

Fire Station No. 2
Issued: 1987 • Retired: 1989

#5461-5

Fisherman's Nook Cabins
Fisherman's Nook Bass Cabin
Issued: 1994 • Current

#5461-5

Fisherman's Nook Cabins
Fisherman's Nook Trout Cabin
Issued: 1994 • Current

#5460-7

Fisherman's Nook Resort
Issued: 1994 • Current

SNOW VILLAGE	Original Price	Status	Market Value	Year Purch.	Price Paid	Value of My Collection
1. English Tudor	$30.00	Retired	$278.00			
2. Farm House	$40.00	Retired	$77.00			
3. Federal House (*American Architecture Series*)	$50.00	Current	$50.00			
4. Finklea's Finery: Costume Shop	$45.00	Retired	$65.00			
5. Fire Station	$32.00	Retired	$635.00			
6. Fire Station No. 2	$40.00	Retired	$215.00			
7. Fisherman's Nook Cabins (set/2)	$50.00	Current	$50.00			
a *Fisherman's Nook Bass Cabin*						
b *Fisherman's Nook Trout Cabin*						
8. Fisherman's Nook Resort	$75.00	Current	$75.00			

✎ **PENCIL TOTALS**

	PRICE PAID	MARKET VALUE

SNOW VILLAGE

#		#5082-2
1	**Flower Shop** Issued: 1982 • Retired: 1983	

Flower Shop
Issued: 1982 • Retired: 1983
#5082-2

2 **Gabled Cottage**
Issued: 1976 • Retired: 1979
#5002-1

3 **Gabled House**
Issued: 1982 • Retired: 1983
#5081-4

4 **Galena House**
Issued: 1984 • Retired: 1985
#5009-1

5 **General Store**
Issued: 1978 • Retired: 1980
#5012-0

6 **Giant Trees**
Issued: 1979 • Retired: 1982
#5065-8

7 **Gingerbread House**
Issued: 1983 • Retired: 1984
Coin bank, non-lit
#5025-3

8 **Glenhaven House**
Issued: 1994 • Current
#5468-2

9 **Good Shepherd Chapel & Church School (set/2)**
Issued: 1992 • Retired: 1996
#5424-0

	SNOW VILLAGE	Original Price	Status	Market Value	Year Purch.	Price Paid	Value of My Collection
1.	Flower Shop	$25.00	Retired	$468.00			
2.	Gabled Cottage	$20.00	Retired	$365.00			
3.	Gabled House	$30.00	Retired	$385.00			
4.	Galena House	$32.00	Retired	$325.00			
5.	General Store	$25.00	Retired	$472.00			
	• Variation: gold			$551.00			
	• Variation: tan			$610.00			
6.	Giant Trees	$20.00	Retired	$346.00			
7.	Gingerbread House (coin bank)	$24.00	Retired	$310.00			
8.	Glenhaven House	$45.00	Current	$45.00			
9.	Good Shepherd Chapel & Church School (set/2)	$72.00	Retired	$93.00			

✎ PENCIL TOTALS

PRICE PAID	MARKET VALUE

#5028-8

Gothic Church
Issued: 1983 • Retired: 1986

#5404-6

Gothic Farmhouse
Issued: 1991 • Current
American Architecture Series

#5003-2

Governor's Mansion
Issued: 1983 • Retired: 1985

#5420-8

Grandma's Cottage
Issued: 1992 • Retired: 1996

#5001-6

Grocery
Issued: 1983 • Retired: 1985

NEW!

#54886

Harley-Davidson Motorcycle Shop
Issued: 1996 • Current

#5426-7

Hartford House
Issued: 1992 • Retired: 1995

#5008-3

Haversham House
Issued: 1984 • Retired: 1987

#5063-6

Highland Park House
Issued: 1986 • Retired: 1988

SNOW VILLAGE	Original Price	Status	Market Value	Year Purch.	Price Paid	Value of My Collection
1. Gothic Church	$36.00	Retired	$270.00			
2. Gothic Farmhouse (*American Architecture Series*)	$48.00	Current	$48.00			
3. Governor's Mansion	$32.00	Retired	$315.00			
4. Grandma's Cottage	$42.00	Retired	$60.00			
5. Grocery	$35.00	Retired	$357.00			
6. Harley-Davidson Motorcycle Shop	$65.00	Current	$65.00			
7. Hartford House	$55.00	Retired	$86.00			
8. Haversham House	$37.00	Retired	$278.00			
9. Highland Park House	$35.00	Retired	$158.00			
			✎ **PENCIL TOTALS**			
					PRICE PAID	MARKET VALUE

SNOW VILLAGE

VALUE GUIDE — SNOW VILLAGE

1 #54854
Holly Brothers Garage
Issued: 1995 • Current

2 #5126-8
**Home Sweet Home/
House & Windmill (set/2)**
Issued: 1988 • Retired: 1991

3 #5011-2
Homestead
Issued: 1978 • Retired: 1984

4 #5401-1
The Honeymooner Motel
Issued: 1991 • Retired: 1993

5 #5445-3
Hunting Lodge
Issued: 1993 • Retired: 1996

6 #5003-9
The Inn
Issued: 1976 • Retired: 1979

7 #5149-7
J. Young's Granary
Issued: 1989 • Retired: 1992

8 #5406-2
Jack's Corner Barber Shop
Issued: 1991 • Retired: 1994

9 #5082-2
Jefferson School
Issued: 1987 • Retired: 1991

	SNOW VILLAGE	Original Price	Status	Market Value	Year Purch.	Price Paid	Value of My Collection
1.	Holly Brothers Garage	$48.00	Current	$48.00			
2.	Home Sweet Home/ House & Windmill (set/2)	$60.00	Retired	$124.00			
3.	Homestead	$30.00	Retired	$261.00			
4.	The Honeymooner Motel	$42.00	Retired	$83.00			
5.	Hunting Lodge	$50.00	Retired	$68.00			
6.	The Inn	$20.00	Retired	$430.00			
7.	J. Young's Granary	$45.00	Retired	$83.00			
8.	Jack's Corner Barber Shop	$42.00	Retired	$72.00			
9.	Jefferson School	$36.00	Retired	$162.00			

✎ **PENCIL TOTALS**

PRICE PAID	MARKET VALUE

#5114-4	#5054-7	#5055-9
1 Jingle Belle Houseboat Issued: 1989 • Retired: 1991	**2** Kenwood House Issued: 1988 • Retired: 1990	**3** Knob Hill Issued: 1979 • Retired: 1981
4 #5080-6 Large Single Tree Issued: 1981 • Retired: 1989	**5** #5030-0 Lighthouse Issued: 1987 • Retired: 1988	**6** #5060-1 Lincoln Park Duplex Issued: 1986 • Retired: 1988
7 #5057-5 Log Cabin Issued: 1979 • Retired: 1981	**8** #5005-9 Main Street House Issued: 1984 • Retired: 1986	**9** #5153-5 Mainstreet Hardware Store Issued: 1990 • Retired: 1993

	SNOW VILLAGE	Original Price	Status	Market Value	Year Purch.	Price Paid	Value of My Collection
1.	Jingle Belle Houseboat	$42.00	Retired	$124.00			
2.	Kenwood House	$50.00	Retired	$138.00			
3.	Knob Hill • Variation: gold	$30.00	Retired	$396.00 $370.00			
4.	Large Single Tree	$17.00	Retired	$48.00			
5.	Lighthouse	$36.00	Retired	$600.00			
6.	Lincoln Park Duplex	$33.00	Retired	$138.00			
7.	Log Cabin	$22.00	Retired	$435.00			
8.	Main Street House	$27.00	Retired	$259.00			
9.	Mainstreet Hardware Store	$42.00	Retired	$80.00			

✎ **PENCIL TOTALS**

Price Paid	Market Value

SNOW VILLAGE

1 — #5008-8 — **Mansion** — Issued: 1977 • Retired: 1979

2 — #5121-7 — **Maple Ridge Inn** — Issued: 1988 • Retired: 1990

3 — #5470-4 — **Marvel's Beauty Salon** — Issued: 1994 • Current

4 — #5062-5 — **Mission Church** — Issued: 1979 • Retired: 1980

5 — #5063-3 — **Mobile Home** — Issued: 1979 • Retired: 1980

6 — #5152-7 — **Morningside House** — Issued: 1990 • Retired: 1992

7 — #5442-9 — **Mount Olivet Church** — Issued: 1993 • Retired: 1996

8 — #5001-3 — **Mountain Lodge** — Issued: 1976 • Retired: 1979

9 — #5014-6 — **Nantucket** — Issued: 1978 • Retired: 1986

	Snow Village	Original Price	Status	Market Value	Year Purch.	Price Paid	Value of My Collection
1.	Mansion	$30.00	Retired	$500.00			
2.	Maple Ridge Inn	$55.00	Retired	$84.00			
3.	Marvel's Beauty Salon	$37.50	Current	$37.50			
4.	Mission Church	$30.00	Retired	$1240.00			
5.	Mobile Home	$18.00	Retired	$1990.00			
6.	Morningside House	$45.00	Retired	$69.00			
7.	Mount Olivet Church	$65.00	Retired	$78.00			
8.	Mountain Lodge	$20.00	Retired	$358.00			
9.	Nantucket	$25.00	Retired	$270.00			
		PENCIL TOTALS				Price Paid	Market Value

#5441-0

(1) Nantucket Renovation
Issued: 1993 • Retired: 1993
Limited to 1993 production

#5037-7

(2) New School House
Issued: 1984 • Retired: 1986

#5083-0

(3) New Stone Church
Issued: 1982 • Retired: 1984

#54871

(4) Nick's Tree Farm (set/10)
Issued: 1996 • Current

#5120-9

(5) North Creek Cottage
Issued: 1989 • Retired: 1992

#5400-3

(6) Oak Grove Tudor
Issued: 1991 • Retired: 1994

#5462-3

(7a) The Original Snow Village
Starter Set
Shady Oak Church
Issued: 1994 • Retired: 1996

#5462-3

(7b) The Original Snow Village
Starter Set
Sunday School Serenade (accessory)
Issued: 1994 • Retired: 1996

#5066-0

(8) Pacific Heights House
Issued: 1986 • Retired: 1988

SNOW VILLAGE		Original Price	Status	Market Value	Year Purch.	Price Paid	Value of My Collection
1.	Nantucket Renovation	$55.00	Retired	$79.00			
2.	New School House	$35.00	Retired	$260.00			
3.	New Stone Church	$32.00	Retired	$387.00			
4.	Nick's Tree Farm (set/10)	$40.00	Current	$40.00			
5.	North Creek Cottage	$45.00	Retired	$74.00			
6.	Oak Grove Tudor	$42.00	Retired	$70.00			
7.	The Original Snow Village Starter Set (set/6) *	$50.00	Retired	$65.00			
a	*Shady Oak Church*						
b	*Sunday School Serenade (accessory)*						
8.	Pacific Heights House	$33.00	Retired	$111.00			
	* the starter set also includes snow and trees, indiv. pricing not established						

✏ PENCIL TOTALS

	PRICE PAID	MARKET VALUE

SNOW VILLAGE

VALUE GUIDE — SNOW VILLAGE

1 #5141-1
Palos Verdes
Issued: 1988 • Retired: 1990

2 #5142-0
Paramount Theater
Issued: 1989 • Retired: 1993

3 #5039-3
Parish Church
Issued: 1984 • Retired: 1986

4 #5029-6
Parsonage
Issued: 1983 • Retired: 1985

5 #5485-2
Peppermint Porch Day Care
Issued: 1995 • Current

6 #5150-0
Pinewood Log Cabin
Issued: 1989 • Retired: 1995

7 #5022-9
Pioneer Church
Issued: 1982 • Retired: 1984

8 #54851
Pisa Pizza
Issued: 1995 • Current

9 #5047-4
Plantation House
Issued: 1985 • Retired: 1987

	SNOW VILLAGE	Original Price	Status	Market Value	Year Purch.	Price Paid	Value of My Collection
1.	Palos Verdes	$37.50	Retired	$83.00			
2.	Paramount Theater	$42.00	Retired	$140.00			
3.	Parish Church	$32.00	Retired	$322.00			
4.	Parsonage	$35.00	Retired	$365.00			
5.	Peppermint Porch Day Care	$45.00	Current	$45.00			
6.	Pinewood Log Cabin	$37.50	Retired	$68.00			
7.	Pioneer Church	$30.00	Retired	$328.00			
8.	Pisa Pizza	$35.00	Current	$35.00			
9.	Plantation House	$37.00	Retired	$123.00			

✏️ **PENCIL TOTALS**

PRICE PAID	MARKET VALUE

1. #5156-0
Prairie House
Issued: 1990 • Retired: 1993
American Architecture Series

2. #5425-9
Print Shop & Village News
Issued: 1992 • Retired: 1994

3. #5157-8
Queen Anne Victorian
Issued: 1990 • Retired: 1996
American Architecture Series

4. #5067-9
Ramsey Hill House
Issued: 1986 • Retired: 1989

5. #5081-4
Red Barn
Issued: 1987 • Retired: 1992

6. #5127-6
Redeemer Church
Issued: 1988 • Retired: 1992

7. #54874
Reindeer Bus Depot
Issued: 1996 • Current

8. #5052-0
Ridgewood
Issued: 1985 • Retired: 1987

9. #5010-5
River Road House
Issued: 1984 • Retired: 1987

	SNOW VILLAGE	Original Price	Status	Market Value	Year Purch.	Price Paid	Value of My Collection
1.	Prairie House (*American Architecture Series*)	$42.00	Retired	$73.00			
2.	Print Shop & Village News	$37.50	Retired	$70.00			
3.	Queen Anne Victorian (*American Architecture Series*)	$48.00	Retired	$66.00			
4.	Ramsey Hill House	$36.00	Retired	$104.00			
5.	Red Barn	$38.00	Retired	$90.00			
6.	Redeemer Church	$42.00	Retired	$71.00			
7.	Reindeer Bus Depot	$42.00	Current	$42.00			
8.	Ridgewood	$35.00	Retired	$172.00			
9.	River Road House	$36.00	Retired	$208.00			

✏ **PENCIL TOTALS**

PRICE PAID	MARKET VALUE

#54880
1
NEW!
Rockabilly Records
Issued: 1996 • Current

#54883
2
NEW!
Rosita's Cantina
Issued: 1996 • Current

#54855
3
Ryman Auditorium
Issued: 1995 • Current

#5006-7
4
St. Anthony Hotel & Post Office
Issued: 1987 • Retired: 1989

#5068-7
5
Saint James Church
Issued: 1986 • Retired: 1988

#5421-6
6
St. Luke's Church
Issued: 1992 • Retired: 1994

#5060-9
7
School House
Issued: 1979 • Retired: 1982

#54885
8
NEW!
The Secret Garden Florist
Issued: 1996 • Current

#5128-4
9
Service Station
Issued: 1988 • Retired: 1991

	SNOW VILLAGE	Original Price	Status	Market Value	Year Purch.	Price Paid	Value of My Collection
1.	Rockabilly Records	$45.00	Current	$45.00			
2.	Rosita's Cantina	$50.00	Current	$50.00			
3.	Ryman Auditorium	$75.00	Current	$75.00			
4.	St. Anthony Hotel & Post Office	$40.00	Retired	$117.00			
5.	Saint James Church	$37.00	Retired	$170.00			
6.	St. Luke's Church	$45.00	Retired	$75.00			
7.	School House	$30.00	Retired	$374.00			
8.	The Secret Garden Florist	$50.00	Current	$50.00			
9.	Service Station	$37.50	Retired	$305.00			

✏️ **PENCIL TOTALS**

PRICE PAID	MARKET VALUE

1 NEW!	#54884	2	#5125-0	3	#5467-4
Shingle Victorian Issued: 1996 • Current *American Architecture Series*		**Single Car Garage** Issued: 1988 • Retired: 1990		**Skate & Ski Shop** Issued: 1994 • Current	
4	#5017-2	5	#5015-3	6	#5006-2
Skating Pond Issued: 1982 • Retired: 1984		**Skating Rink/Duck Pond Set** Issued: 1978 • Retired: 1979		**Small Chalet** Issued: 1976 • Retired: 1979	
7	#5016-1	8	#54872	9	#54850
Small Double Trees Issued: 1978 • Retired: 1989		**Smokey Mountain Retreat (w/smoking chimney)** Issued: 1996 • Current		**Snow Carnival Ice Palace (set/2)** Issued: 1995 • Current	

	SNOW VILLAGE	Original Price	Status	Market Value	Year Purch.	Price Paid	Value of My Collection
1.	Shingle Victorian *(American Architecture Series)*	$55.00	Current	$55.00			
2.	Single Car Garage	$22.00	Retired	$60.00			
3.	Skate & Ski Shop	$50.00	Current	$50.00			
4.	Skating Pond	$25.00	Retired	$366.00			
5.	Skating Rink/Duck Pond Set	$16.00	Retired	$1000.00			
6.	Small Chalet	$15.00	Retired	$440.00			
7.	Small Double Trees • Variation: w/red birds	$13.50	Retired	$185.00 $52.00			
8.	Smokey Mountain Retreat (w/smoking chimney)	$65.00	Current	$65.00			
9.	Snow Carnival Ice Palace (set/2)	$95.00	Current	$95.00			
	✎ **PENCIL TOTALS**					PRICE PAID	MARKET VALUE

VALUE GUIDE — SNOW VILLAGE

1 #5013-0
Snow Village Factory
Issued: 1987 • Retired: 1989

2 #5092-0
Snow Village Resort Lodge
Issued: 1987 • Retired: 1989

3 #5448-8
Snowy Hills Hospital
Issued: 1993 • Retired: 1996

4 #5062-8
Sonoma House
Issued: 1986 • Retired: 1988

5 #5403-8
Southern Colonial
Issued: 1991 • Retired: 1994
American Architecture Series

6 #5155-1
Spanish Mission Church
Issued: 1990 • Retired: 1992

7 #5027-0
Springfield House
Issued: 1987 • Retired: 1990

8 #5049-0
Spruce Place
Issued: 1985 • Retired: 1987

9 #54859
Starbucks Coffee
Issued: 1995 • Current

	SNOW VILLAGE	Original Price	Status	Market Value	Year Purch.	Price Paid	Value of My Collection
1.	Snow Village Factory	$45.00	Retired	$138.00			
2.	Snow Village Resort Lodge	$55.00	Retired	$150.00			
3.	Snowy Hills Hospital	$48.00	Retired	$72.00			
4.	Sonoma House	$33.00	Retired	$146.00			
5.	Southern Colonial (*American Architecture Series*)	$50.00	Retired	$76.00			
6.	Spanish Mission Church	$42.00	Retired	$80.00			
7.	Springfield House	$40.00	Retired	$82.00			
8.	Spruce Place	$33.00	Retired	$283.00			
9.	Starbucks Coffee	$48.00	Current	$48.00			

✎ **PENCIL TOTALS**

	PRICE PAID	MARKET VALUE

Snow Village	Original Price	Status	Market Value	Year Purch.	Price Paid	Value of My Collection
1. Steepled Church	$25.00	Retired	$555.00			
2. Stone Church (1977)	$35.00	Retired	$580.00			
3. Stone Church (1979)	$32.00	Retired	$970.00			
4. Stone Mill House	$30.00	Retired	$500.00			
5. Stonehurst House	$37.50	Retired	$66.00			
6. Stratford House	$28.00	Retired	$180.00			
7. Street Car	$16.00	Retired	$380.00			
8. Stucco Bungalow	$30.00	Retired	$367.00			
9. Summit House	$28.00	Retired	$352.00			
			✏️ **PENCIL TOTALS**			
					Price Paid	Market Value

1 #5023-7 — **Swiss Chalet** — Issued: 1982 • Retired: 1984

2 #5071-7 — **Town Church** — Issued: 1980 • Retired: 1982

3 #5000-8 — **Town Hall** — Issued: 1983 • Retired: 1984

4 #5073-3 — **Toy Shop** — Issued: 1986 • Retired: 1990

5 #5085-6 — **Train Station With 3 Train Cars (set/4)** — Issued: 1980 • Retired: 1985

6 #54890 NEW! — **Treetop Tree House** — Issued: 1996 • Current

7 #5035-0 — **Trinity Church** — Issued: 1984 • Retired: 1986

8 #5061-7 — **Tudor House** — Issued: 1979 • Retired: 1981

9 #5004-0 — **Turn Of The Century** — Issued: 1983 • Retired: 1986

	SNOW VILLAGE	Original Price	Status	Market Value	Year Purch.	Price Paid	Value of My Collection
1.	Swiss Chalet	$28.00	Retired	$430.00			
2.	Town Church	$33.00	Retired	$362.00			
3.	Town Hall	$32.00	Retired	$358.00			
4.	Toy Shop	$36.00	Retired	$97.00			
5.	Train Station With 3 Train Cars (set/4) • Variation: 6 window panes, round window in door • Variation: 8 window panes, 2 square windows in door	$100.00	Retired	---- $390.00 $340.00			
6.	Treetop Tree House	$35.00	Current	$35.00			
7.	Trinity Church	$32.00	Retired	$290.00			
8.	Tudor House	$25.00	Retired	$302.00			
9.	Turn Of The Century	$36.00	Retired	$258.00			

✎ **PENCIL TOTALS**

PRICE PAID	MARKET VALUE

	#5042-3		#5054-2		#5002-4
1 Twin Peaks Issued: 1986 • Retired: 1986		**2** Victorian Issued: 1979 • Retired: 1982		**3** Victorian Cottage Issued: 1983 • Retired: 1984	
	#5007-0		#5026-1		#5402-0
4 Victorian House Issued: 1977 • Retired: 1979		**5** Village Church Issued: 1983 • Retired: 1984		**6** Village Greenhouse Issued: 1991 • Retired: 1995	
	#5044-0		#54853		#5422-4
7 Village Market Issued: 1988 • Retired: 1991		**8** Village Police Station Issued: 1995 • Current		**9** Village Post Office Issued: 1992 • Retired: 1995	

	SNOW VILLAGE	Original Price	Status	Market Value	Year Purch.	Price Paid	Value of My Collection
1.	Twin Peaks	$32.00	Retired	$480.00			
2.	Victorian	$30.00	Retired	$340.00			
3.	Victorian Cottage	$35.00	Retired	$350.00			
4.	Victorian House	$30.00	Retired	$440.00			
5.	Village Church	$30.00	Retired	$400.00			
6.	Village Greenhouse	$35.00	Retired	$63.00			
7.	Village Market	$39.00	Retired	$79.00			
8.	Village Police Station	$48.00	Current	$48.00			
9.	Village Post Office	$35.00	Retired	$72.00			
		✎ PENCIL TOTALS				PRICE PAID	MARKET VALUE

SNOW VILLAGE

1 #5443-7
Village Public Library
Issued: 1993 • Current

2 #5154-3
Village Realty
Issued: 1990 • Retired: 1993

3 #5438-0
Village Station
Issued: 1992 • Current

4 #5122-5
Village Station And Train (set/2)
Issued: 1988 • Retired: 1992

5 #5427-5
Village Vet And Pet Shop
Issued: 1992 • Retired: 1995

6 #5145-4
Village Warming House
Issued: 1989 • Retired: 1992

7 #5041-5
Waverly Place
Issued: 1986 • Retired: 1986

8 #5464-0
Wedding Chapel
Issued: 1994 • Current

9 #5046-6
Williamsburg House
Issued: 1985 • Retired: 1988

	SNOW VILLAGE	Original Price	Status	Market Value	Year Purch.	Price Paid	Value of My Collection
1.	Village Public Library	$55.00	Current	$55.00			
2.	Village Realty	$42.00	Retired	$78.00			
3.	Village Station	$65.00	Current	$65.00			
4.	Village Station And Train (set/2)	$65.00	Retired	$108.00			
5.	Village Vet And Pet Shop	$32.00	Retired	$65.00			
6.	Village Warming House	$42.00	Retired	$74.00			
7.	Waverly Place	$35.00	Retired	$305.00			
8.	Wedding Chapel	$55.00	Current	$55.00			
9.	Williamsburg House	$37.00	Retired	$152.00			

PENCIL TOTALS

PRICE PAID	MARKET VALUE

	#5444-5		#5031-8		#5072-5
1	**Woodbury House** Issued: 1993 • Retired: 1996	**2**	**Wooden Church** Issued: 1983 • Retired: 1985	**3**	**Wooden Clapboard** Issued: 1981 • Retired: 1984

	SNOW VILLAGE	Original Price	Status	Market Value	Year Purch.	Price Paid	Value of My Collection
1.	Woodbury House	$45.00	Retired	$59.00			
2.	Wooden Church	$30.00	Retired	$354.00			
3.	Wooden Clapboard	$32.00	Retired	$238.00			
		✏ PENCIL TOTALS				PRICE PAID	MARKET VALUE

SNOW VILLAGE

Use this page to record future Snow Village buildings.

SNOW VILLAGE	Original Price	Status	Market Value	Year Purch.	Price Paid	Value of My Collection
				PENCIL TOTALS		
					PRICE PAID	MARKET VALUE

#5102-0

(1)

#5129-2

(2)

#5055-5

(3)

3 Nuns With Songbooks
Issued: 1987 • Retired: 1988

Apple Girl/Newspaper Boy (set/2)
Issued: 1988 • Retired: 1990

Auto With Tree
Issued: 1985 • Current

#5169-1

(4)

#5174-8

(5)

#5064-1

(6)

Bringing Home The Tree
Issued: 1989 • Retired: 1992

Calling All Cars (set/2)
Issued: 1989 • Retired: 1991

Carolers (set/4)
Issued: 1979 • Retired: 1986

#5463-1

(7)

#5105-5

(8)

#54896

(9)

NEW!

Caroling At The Farm
Issued: 1994 • Current

Caroling Family (set/3)
Issued: 1987 • Retired: 1990

Caroling Through The Snow
Issued: 1996 • Current

ACCESSORIES SNOW VILLAGE	Original Price	Status	Market Value	Year Purch.	Price Paid	Value of My Collection
1. 3 Nuns With Songbooks	$6.00	Retired	$136.00			
2. Apple Girl/Newspaper Boy (set/2)	$11.00	Retired	$25.00			
3. Auto With Tree	$5.00	Current	$6.50			
4. Bringing Home The Tree	$15.00	Retired	$30.00			
5. Calling All Cars (set/2)	$15.00	Retired	$43.00			
6. Carolers (set/4)	$12.00	Retired	$133.00			
7. Caroling At The Farm	$35.00	Current	$35.00			
8. Caroling Family (set/3)	$20.00	Retired	$32.00			
9. Caroling Through The Snow	$15.00	Current	$15.00			
✎ PENCIL TOTALS					PRICE PAID	MARKET VALUE

ACCESSORIES
SNOW VILLAGE

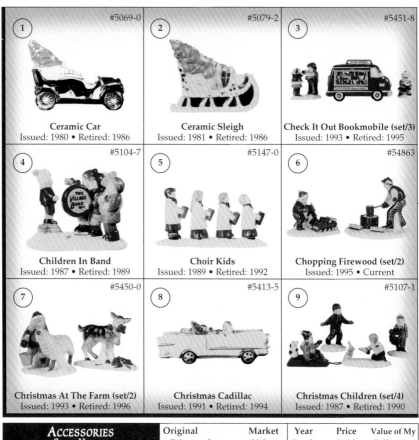

	#5069-0		#5079-2		#5451-8
1		**2**		**3**	
Ceramic Car		**Ceramic Sleigh**		**Check It Out Bookmobile (set/3)**	
Issued: 1980 • Retired: 1986		Issued: 1981 • Retired: 1986		Issued: 1993 • Retired: 1995	

(Row 1: Ceramic Car #5069-0; Ceramic Sleigh #5079-2; Check It Out Bookmobile (set/3) #5451-8)

(Row 2)
- #5104-7 — **4** — **Children In Band** — Issued: 1987 • Retired: 1989
- #5147-0 — **5** — **Choir Kids** — Issued: 1989 • Retired: 1992
- #54863 — **6** — **Chopping Firewood (set/2)** — Issued: 1995 • Current

(Row 3)
- #5450-0 — **7** — **Christmas At The Farm (set/2)** — Issued: 1993 • Retired: 1996
- #5413-5 — **8** — **Christmas Cadillac** — Issued: 1991 • Retired: 1994
- #5107-1 — **9** — **Christmas Children (set/4)** — Issued: 1987 • Retired: 1990

	Accessories Snow Village	Original Price	Status	Market Value	Year Purch.	Price Paid	Value of My Collection
1.	Ceramic Car	$5.00	Retired	$55.00			
2.	Ceramic Sleigh	$5.00	Retired	$60.00			
3.	Check It Out Bookmobile (set/3)	$25.00	Retired	$38.00			
4.	Children In Band	$15.00	Retired	$30.00			
5.	Choir Kids	$15.00	Retired	$29.00			
6.	Chopping Firewood (set/2)	$16.50	Current	$16.50			
7.	Christmas At The Farm (set/2)	$16.00	Retired	$26.00			
8.	Christmas Cadillac	$9.00	Retired	$16.00			
9.	Christmas Children (set/4)	$20.00	Retired	$32.00			
	✎ **PENCIL TOTALS**					Price Paid	Market Value

#5432-1	#5209-4	#5457-7
1 Christmas Puppies (set/2) Issued: 1992 • Retired: 1996	**2** Christmas Trash Cans (set/2) Issued: 1990 • Current	**3** Classic Cars (set/3) Issued: 1993 • Current

#5481-0	#5480-1	#5479-8
4 Coca-Cola® Brand Billboard Issued: 1994 • Current	**5** Coca-Cola® Brand Delivery Men (set/2) Issued: 1994 • Current	**6** Coca-Cola® Brand Delivery Truck Issued: 1994 • Current

#5410-0	#5411-9	#5415-1
7 Cold Weather Sports (set/4) Issued: 1991 • Retired: 1994	**8** Come Join The Parade Issued: 1991 • Retired: 1992	**9** Country Harvest Issued: 1991 • Retired: 1993

	ACCESSORIES SNOW VILLAGE	Original Price	Status	Market Value	Year Purch.	Price Paid	Value of My Collection
1.	Christmas Puppies (set/2)	$27.50	Retired	$43.00			
2.	Christmas Trash Cans (set/2)	$6.50	Current	$7.00			
3.	Classic Cars (set/3)	$22.50	Current	$22.50			
4.	Coca-Cola® Brand Billboard	$18.00	Current	$18.00			
5.	Coca-Cola® Brand Delivery Men (set/2)	$25.00	Current	$25.00			
6.	Coca-Cola® Brand Delivery Truck	$15.00	Current	$15.00			
7.	Cold Weather Sports (set/4)	$27.50	Retired	$47.00			
8.	Come Join The Parade	$12.50	Retired	$23.00			
9.	Country Harvest	$13.00	Retired	$26.00			
				PENCIL TOTALS		PRICE PAID	MARKET VALUE

ACCESSORIES
SNOW VILLAGE

1 #5171-3
Crack The Whip (set/3)
Issued: 1989 • Retired: 1996

2 #5131-4
Doghouse/Cat In Garbage Can (set/2)
Issued: 1988 • Retired: 1992

3 #5158-6
Down The Chimney He Goes
Issued: 1990 • Retired: 1993

4 #5431-3
Early Morning Delivery (set/3)
Issued: 1992 • Retired: 1995

5 #5057-1
Family Mom/Kids, Goose/Girl (set/2)
Issued: 1985 • Retired: 1988

6 #5473-9
Feeding The Birds (set/3)
Issued: 1994 • Current

7 #5132-2
Fire Hydrant And Mailbox (set/2)
Issued: 1988 • Current

8 #54864
Firewood Delivery Truck
Issued: 1995 • Current

9 #5177-2
Flag Pole
Issued: 1989 • Current

	ACCESSORIES SNOW VILLAGE	Original Price	Status	Market Value	Year Purch.	Price Paid	Value of My Collection
1.	Crack The Whip (set/3)	$25.00	Retired	$34.00			
2.	Doghouse/Cat In Garbage Can (set/2)	$15.00	Retired	$29.00			
3.	Down The Chimney He Goes	$6.50	Retired	$17.00			
4.	Early Morning Delivery (set/3)	$27.50	Retired	$36.00			
5.	Family Mom/Kids, Goose/Girl (set/2)	$11.00	Retired	$45.00			
6.	Feeding The Birds (set/3)	$25.00	Current	$25.00			
7.	Fire Hydrant And Mailbox (set/2)	$6.00	Current	$6.00			
8.	Firewood Delivery Truck	$15.00	Current	$15.00			
9.	Flag Pole	$8.50	Current	$8.50			

PENCIL TOTALS

PRICE PAID	MARKET VALUE

#5108-0 (1)
For Sale Sign
Issued: 1987 • Retired: 1989

#5166-7 (2)
For Sale Sign
Issued: 1989 • Current

#5163-2 (3)
Fresh Frozen Fish (set/2)
Issued: 1990 • Retired: 1993

#54860 (4)
Frosty Playtime (set/3)
Issued: 1995 • Current

#5095-4 (5)
Girl/Snowman, Boy (set/2)
Issued: 1986 • Retired: 1987

#5476-3 (6)
Going To The Chapel (set/2)
Issued: 1994 • Current

#54867 (7)
Grand Ole Opry Carolers
Issued: 1995 • Current

#54900 (8) NEW!
Harley-Davidson Fat Boy & Softail
Issued: 1996 • Current

#54898 (9) NEW!
A Harley-Davidson Holiday (set/2)
Issued: 1996 • Current

	ACCESSORIES SNOW VILLAGE	Original Price	Status	Market Value	Year Purch.	Price Paid	Value of My Collection
1.	For Sale Sign	$3.50	Retired	$13.00			
	• Variation: blank sign, #581-9			$15.00			
2.	For Sale Sign	$4.50	Current	$4.50			
	• Variation: Bachman's Village Gathering Sign (1990)			$22.00			
3.	Fresh Frozen Fish (set/2)	$20.00	Retired	$39.00			
4.	Frosty Playtime (set/3)	$30.00	Current	$30.00			
5.	Girl/Snowman, Boy (set/2)	$11.00	Retired	$67.00			
6.	Going To The Chapel (set/2)	$20.00	Current	$20.00			
7.	Grand Ole Opry Carolers	$25.00	Current	$25.00			
8.	Harley-Davidson Fat Boy & Softail	$16.50	Current	$16.50			
9.	A Harley-Davidson Holiday (set/2)	$22.50	Current	$22.50			

✎ **PENCIL TOTALS**

PRICE PAID	MARKET VALUE

1 NEW! #54901
Harley-Davidson Sign
Issued: 1996 • Current

2 #5117-9
Hayride
Issued: 1988 • Retired: 1990

3 NEW! #54897
Heading For The Hills (2 asst.)
Issued: 1996 • Current

4 #5434-8
A Heavy Snowfall (set/2)
Issued: 1992 • Current

5 #5455-0
A Herd Of Holiday Heifers
(set/3)
Issued: 1993 • Current

6 various
Here Comes Santa
Issued: 1996 • Retired
Limited to 1996 production

7 #5161-6
Here We Come A Caroling
(set/3)
Issued: 1990 • Retired: 1992

8 NEW! #54893
Holiday Hoops (set/3)
Issued: 1996 • Current

9 #5162-4
Home Delivery (set/2)
Issued: 1990 • Retired: 1992

	ACCESSORIES SNOW VILLAGE	Original Price	Status	Market Value	Year Purch.	Price Paid	Value of My Collection
1.	Harley-Davidson Sign	$18.00	Current	$18.00			
2.	Hayride	$30.00	Retired	$65.00			
3.	Heading For The Hills (2 asst.)	$8.50	Current	$8.50			
4.	A Heavy Snowfall (set/2)	$16.00	Current	$16.00			
5.	A Herd Of Holiday Heifers (set/3)	$18.00	Current	$18.00			
6.	Here Comes Santa	$25.00	Retired	not established			
	• Variations: Bachman's; Bronner's; Broughton Christmas Shop; Cabbage Rose; Calabash; Calico Butterfly; Carson Pirie Scott; The Christmas Loft; Dickens Gift Shop; European Imports; Fibber Magee's; Fortunoff; Gustaf's; Ingle's Nook; The Limited Edition; North Pole City; Pine Cone Shop; Royal Dutch; Russ Country Gardens; St. Nick's; Seventh Avenue; Stats; William Glen; Young's Ltd.						
7.	Here We Come A Caroling (set/3)	$18.00	Retired	$28.00			
8.	Holiday Hoops (set/3)	$20.00	Current	$20.00			
9.	Home Delivery (set/2)	$16.00	Retired	$31.00			

✎ **PENCIL TOTALS**

PRICE PAID	MARKET VALUE

1 #5165-9
A Home For The Holidays
Issued: 1990 • Retired: 1996

2 #54879
Just Married (set/2)
Issued: 1995 • Current

3 #5094-6
Kids Around The Tree
Issued: 1986 • Retired: 1990

4 #5134-9
Kids Decorating The Village Sign
Issued: 1990 • Retired: 1993

5 #5168-3
Kids Tree House
Issued: 1989 • Retired: 1991

6 #5179-9
Mailbox
Issued: 1989 • Retired: 1990

7 #5198-5
Mailbox
Issued: 1990 • Current

8 #5116-0
Man On Ladder Hanging Garland
Issued: 1988 • Retired: 1992

9 #5478-0
Marshmallow Roast (set/3)
Issued: 1994 • Current

	ACCESSORIES SNOW VILLAGE	Original Price	Status	Market Value	Year Purch.	Price Paid	Value of My Collection
1.	A Home For The Holidays	$6.50	Retired	$15.00			
2.	Just Married (set/2)	$25.00	Current	$25.00			
3.	Kids Around The Tree	$15.00	Retired	$64.00			
	• Variation: smaller			$43.00			
4.	Kids Decorating The Village Sign	$12.50	Retired	$25.00			
5.	Kids Tree House	$25.00	Retired	$51.00			
6.	Mailbox (red, white & blue)	$3.50	Retired	$18.00			
7.	Mailbox (red & green)	$3.50	Current	$3.50			
8.	Man On Ladder Hanging Garland	$7.50	Retired	$19.00			
9.	Marshmallow Roast (set/3)	$32.50	Current	$32.50			
	PENCIL TOTALS					Price Paid	Market Value

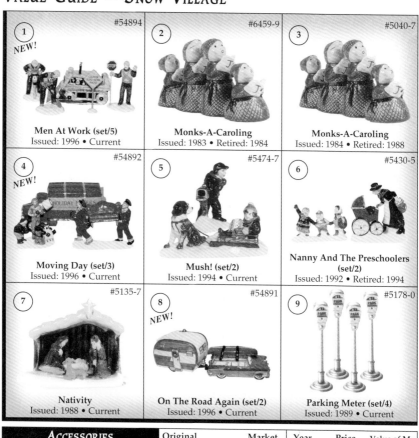

#54894
1 NEW!
Men At Work (set/5)
Issued: 1996 • Current

#6459-9
2
Monks-A-Caroling
Issued: 1983 • Retired: 1984

#5040-7
3
Monks-A-Caroling
Issued: 1984 • Retired: 1988

#54892
4 NEW!
Moving Day (set/3)
Issued: 1996 • Current

#5474-7
5
Mush! (set/2)
Issued: 1994 • Current

#5430-5
6
Nanny And The Preschoolers (set/2)
Issued: 1992 • Retired: 1994

#5135-7
7
Nativity
Issued: 1988 • Current

#54891
8 NEW!
On The Road Again (set/2)
Issued: 1996 • Current

#5178-0
9
Parking Meter (set/4)
Issued: 1989 • Current

	ACCESSORIES SNOW VILLAGE	Original Price	Status	Market Value	Year Purch.	Price Paid	Value of My Collection
1.	Men At Work (set/5)	$27.50	Current	$27.50			
2.	Monks-A-Caroling (#6459-9)	$6.00	Retired	$67.00			
3.	Monks-A-Caroling (#5040-7)	$6.00	Retired	$42.00			
4.	Moving Day (set/3)	$32.50	Current	$32.50			
5.	Mush! (set/2)	$20.00	Current	$20.00			
6.	Nanny And The Preschoolers (set/2)	$27.50	Retired	$37.00			
7.	Nativity	$7.50	Current	$7.50			
8.	On The Road Again (set/2)	$20.00	Current	$20.00			
9.	Parking Meter (set/4)	$6.00	Current	$6.00			

✏️ **PENCIL TOTALS**

PRICE PAID	MARKET VALUE

| | 1 | #5472-0 Pets On Parade (set/2) Issued: 1994 • Current | 2 | #5454-2 Pick-Up And Delivery Issued: 1993 • Current | 3 | #5453-4 Pint-Size Pony Rides (set/3) Issued: 1993 • Retired: 1996 |

#5472-0	#5454-2	#5453-4
1 Pets On Parade (set/2) Issued: 1994 • Current	**2** Pick-Up And Delivery Issued: 1993 • Current	**3** Pint-Size Pony Rides (set/3) Issued: 1993 • Retired: 1996
#54866	#54861	#5103-9
4 Pizza Delivery (set/2) Issued: 1995 • Current	**5** Poinsettias For Sale (set/3) Issued: 1995 • Current	**6** Praying Monks Issued: 1987 • Retired: 1988
#54875	#5433-0	#5449-6
7 A Ride On The Reindeer Lines (set/3) Issued: 1996 • Current	**8** Round & Round We Go! (set/2) Issued: 1992 • Retired: 1995	**9** Safety Patrol (set/4) Issued: 1993 • Current

	ACCESSORIES Snow Village	Original Price	Status	Market Value	Year Purch.	Price Paid	Value of My Collection
1.	Pets On Parade (set/2)	$16.50	Current	$16.50			
2.	Pick-Up And Delivery	$10.00	Current	$10.00			
3.	Pint-Size Pony Rides (set/3)	$37.50	Retired	$42.00			
4.	Pizza Delivery (set/2)	$20.00	Current	$20.00			
5.	Poinsettias For Sale (set/3)	$30.00	Current	$30.00			
6.	Praying Monks	$6.00	Retired	$46.00			
7.	A Ride On The Reindeer Lines (set/3)	$35.00	Current	$35.00			
8.	Round & Round We Go! (set/2)	$18.00	Retired	$30.00			
9.	Safety Patrol (set/4)	$27.50	Current	$27.50			

✎ **PENCIL TOTALS**

Price Paid	Market Value

	ACCESSORIES SNOW VILLAGE	Original Price	Status	Market Value	Year Purch.	Price Paid	Value of My Collection
1.	Santa Comes To Town, 1995	$30.00	Retired	$43.00			
2.	Santa Comes To Town, 1996	$32.50	Retired	$38.00			
3.	Santa Comes To Town, 1997	$35.00	Current	$35.00			
4.	Santa/Mailbox (set/2)	$11.00	Retired	$49.00			
5.	School Bus, Snow Plow (set/2)	$16.00	Retired	$55.00			
6.	School Children (set/3)	$15.00	Retired	$28.00			
7.	Scottie With Tree	$3.00	Retired	$183.00			
8.	Service With A Smile (set/2)	$25.00	Current	$25.00			
9.	Shopping Girls With Packages (set/2)	$11.00	Retired	$50.00			

PENCIL TOTALS

	PRICE PAID	MARKET VALUE

#5053-9	#8183-3	#5170-5
Singing Nuns Issued: 1985 • Retired: 1987	**Sisal Tree Lot** Issued: 1988 • Retired: 1991	**Skate Faster Mom** Issued: 1989 • Retired: 1991

#5475-5	#5160-8	#5159-4
Skaters & Skiers (set/3) Issued: 1994 • Current	**Sleighride** Issued: 1990 • Retired: 1992	**Sno-Jet Snowmobile** Issued: 1990 • Retired: 1993

#54868	#54869	#5113-6
Snow Carnival Ice Sculptures (set/2) Issued: 1995 • Current	**Snow Carnival King & Queen** Issued: 1995 • Current	**Snow Kids (set/4)** Issued: 1987 • Retired: 1990

	ACCESSORIES SNOW VILLAGE	Original Price	Status	Market Value	Year Purch.	Price Paid	Value of My Collection
1.	Singing Nuns	$6.00	Retired	$133.00			
2.	Sisal Tree Lot	$45.00	Retired	$90.00			
3.	Skate Faster Mom	$13.00	Retired	$27.00			
4.	Skaters & Skiers (set/3)	$27.50	Current	$27.50			
5.	Sleighride	$30.00	Retired	$57.00			
6.	Sno-Jet Snowmobile	$15.00	Retired	$26.00			
7.	Snow Carnival Ice Sculptures (set/2)	$27.50	Current	$27.50			
8.	Snow Carnival King & Queen	$35.00	Current	$35.00			
9.	Snow Kids (set/4)	$20.00	Retired	$48.00			

✏ **PENCIL TOTALS**

PRICE PAID	MARKET VALUE

ACCESSORIES
SNOW VILLAGE

1 #5056-3

Snow Kids Sled, Skis (set/2)
Issued: 1985 • Retired: 1987

2 #9948-1

Snow Village Promotional Sign
Issued: 1989 • Retired: 1990

3 #5414-3

Snowball Fort (set/3)
Issued: 1991 • Retired: 1993

4 #5018-0

Snowman With Broom
Issued: 1982 • Retired: 1990

5 #5148-9

Special Delivery (set/2)
Issued: 1989 • Retired: 1990
Red, white & blue

6 #5197-7

Special Delivery (set/2)
Issued: 1990 • Retired: 1992
Red & green

7 #5440-2

Spirit Of Snow Village Airplane
Issued: 1992 • Retired: 1996
Red

8a #5458-5

Spirit Of Snow Village Airplane
Issued: 1993 • Retired: 1996
Blue

8b #5458-5

Spirit Of Snow Village Airplane
Issued: 1993 • Retired: 1996
Yellow

	ACCESSORIES SNOW VILLAGE	Original Price	Status	Market Value	Year Purch.	Price Paid	Value of My Collection
1.	Snow Kids Sled, Skis (set/2)	$11.00	Retired	$53.00			
2.	Snow Village Promotional Sign	N/C	Retired	$20.00			
3.	Snowball Fort (set/3)	$27.50	Retired	$42.00			
4.	Snowman With Broom	$3.00	Retired	$14.00			
5.	Special Delivery (set/2, red, white & blue)	$16.00	Retired	$44.00			
6.	Special Delivery (set/2, red & green)	$16.00	Retired	$35.00			
7.	Spirit of Snow Village Airplane	$32.50	Retired	$43.00			
8.	Spirit of Snow Village Airplane (2 assorted)	----	Retired	----			
a	*Blue*	$12.50	Retired	$17.00			
b	*Yellow*	$12.50	Retired	$17.00			

PENCIL TOTALS

PRICE PAID	MARKET VALUE

1	Starbucks Coffee Cart (set/2) #54870 Issued: 1995 • Current
2	Statue Of Mark Twain #5173-0 Issued: 1989 • Retired: 1991
3	Stop Sign (set/2) #5176-4 Issued: 1989 • Current
4	Street Sign (set/6) #5167-5 Issued: 1989 • Retired: 1992
5	Stuck In The Snow (set/3) #5471-2 Issued: 1994 • Current
6	Taxi Cab #5106-3 Issued: 1987 • Current
7	NEW! Terry's Towing (set/2) #54895 Issued: 1996 • Current
8	Through The Woods (set/2) #5172-1 Issued: 1989 • Retired: 1991
9	Tour The Village #5452-6 Issued: 1993 • Current

	ACCESSORIES SNOW VILLAGE	Original Price	Status	Market Value	Year Purch.	Price Paid	Value of My Collection
1.	Starbucks Coffee Cart (set/2)	$27.50	Current	$27.50			
2.	Statue Of Mark Twain	$15.00	Retired	$33.00			
3.	Stop Sign (set/2)	$5.00	Current	$5.00			
4.	Street Sign (set/6)	$7.50	Retired	$12.00			
5.	Stuck In The Snow (set/3)	$30.00	Current	$30.00			
6.	Taxi Cab	$6.00	Current	$6.50			
7.	Terry's Towing (set/2)	$20.00	Current	$20.00			
8.	Through The Woods (set/2)	$18.00	Retired	$28.00			
9.	Tour The Village	$12.50	Current	$12.50			
	PENCIL TOTALS					PRICE PAID	MARKET VALUE

ACCESSORIES
SNOW VILLAGE

#5164-0
(1)
A Tree For Me (set/2)
Issued: 1990 • Retired: 1995

#5138-1
(2)
Tree Lot
Issued: 1988 • Current

#5139-0
(3)
Up On A Roof Top
Issued: 1988 • Current

#52593
(4)
Up, Up & Away
Issued: 1995 • Current

#52642
(5) NEW!
Village Animated Accessory Track
Issued: 1996 • Current

#5247-7
(6)
Village Animated All Around The Park (set/18)
Issued: 1994 • Retired: 1996

#5229-9
(7)
Village Animated Skating Pond (set/15)
Issued: 1993 • Current

#52641
(8) NEW!
Village Animated Ski Mountain
Issued: 1996 • Current

#5180-2
(9)
Village Birds (set/6)
Issued: 1989 • Retired: 1994

	ACCESSORIES SNOW VILLAGE	Original Price	Status	Market Value	Year Purch.	Price Paid	Value of My Collection
1.	A Tree For Me (set/2)	$7.50	Retired	$12.00			
2.	Tree Lot	$33.50	Current	$37.50			
3.	Up On A Roof Top	$6.50	Current	$6.50			
4.	Up, Up & Away	$40.00	Current	$40.00			
5.	Village Animated Accessory Track	$65.00	Current	$65.00			
6.	Village Animated All Around The Park (set/18)	$95.00	Retired	$100.00			
7.	Village Animated Skating Pond (set/15)	$60.00	Current	$60.00			
8.	Village Animated Ski Mountain	$75.00	Current	$75.00			
9.	Village Birds (set/6)	$3.50	Retired	$10.00			
			PENCIL TOTALS			PRICE PAID	MARKET VALUE

#5146-2
1
Village Gazebo
Issued: 1989 • Retired: 1995

#5418-6
2
Village Greetings (set/3)
Issued: 1991 • Retired: 1994

#5412-7
3
Village Marching Band (set/3)
Issued: 1991 • Retired: 1992

#5459-3
4
Village News Delivery (set/2)
Issued: 1993 • Retired: 1996

#5429-1
5
Village Phone Booth
Issued: 1992 • Current

#5192-6
6
Village Potted Topiary Pair
Issued: 1989 • Retired: 1994

#5240-0
7
Village Streetcar (set/10)
Issued: 1994 • Current

#5428-3
8
Village Used Car Lot (set/5)
Issued: 1992 • Current

#52644
9
NEW!
Village Waterfall
Issued: 1996 • Current

	ACCESSORIES SNOW VILLAGE	Original Price	Status	Market Value	Year Purch.	Price Paid	Value of My Collection
1.	Village Gazebo	$27.00	Retired	$45.00			
2.	Village Greetings (set/3)	$5.00	Retired	$10.00			
3.	Village Marching Band (set/3)	$30.00	Retired	$57.00			
4.	Village News Delivery (set/2)	$15.00	Retired	$25.00			
5.	Village Phone Booth	$7.50	Current	$7.50			
6.	Village Potted Topiary Pair	$5.00	Retired	$6.00			
7.	Village Streetcar (set/10)	$65.00	Current	$65.00			
8.	Village Used Car Lot (set/5)	$45.00	Current	$45.00			
9.	Village Waterfall	$65.00	Current	$65.00			

✎ **PENCIL TOTALS**

PRICE PAID	MARKET VALUE

ACCESSORIES
SNOW VILLAGE

1 various	**2** #5133-0	**3** #5435-6
A Visit With Santa Issued: 1995 • Retired: 1995	**Water Tower** Issued: 1988 • Retired: 1991	**We're Going To A Christmas Pageant** Issued: 1992 • Retired: 1994
4 #5456-9	**5** #5409-7	**6** #5436-4
Windmill Issued: 1993 • Current	**Winter Fountain** Issued: 1991 • Retired: 1993	**Winter Playground** Issued: 1992 • Retired: 1995
7 #5130-6	**8** #5136-5	**9** #5408-9
Woodsman And Boy (set/2) Issued: 1988 • Retired: 1991	**Woody Station Wagon** Issued: 1988 • Retired: 1990	**Wreaths For Sale (set/4)** Issued: 1991 • Retired: 1994

	ACCESSORIES SNOW VILLAGE	Original Price	Status	Market Value	Year Purch.	Price Paid	Value of My Collection
1.	A Visit With Santa	$25.00	Retired	see below			
	• Variations: Bachman's - $60; Fortunoff - $65; Lemon Tree - $65; Limited Edition - $75; The Pine Cone Shop - $60; Stats - $65; William Glen - $65; Young's Limited Edition - $60.						
2.	Water Tower	$20.00	Retired	$74.00			
	• Variation: "Moline, Home Of John Deere"			$690.00			
3.	We're Going To A Christmas Pageant	$15.00	Retired	$23.00			
4.	Windmill	$20.00	Current	$20.00			
5.	Winter Fountain	$25.00	Retired	$54.00			
6.	Winter Playground	$20.00	Retired	$34.00			
7.	Woodsman And Boy (set/2)	$13.00	Retired	$29.00			
8.	Woody Station Wagon	$6.50	Retired	$30.00			
9.	Wreaths For Sale (set/4)	$27.50	Retired	$43.00			

✎ **PENCIL TOTALS**

Price Paid	Market Value

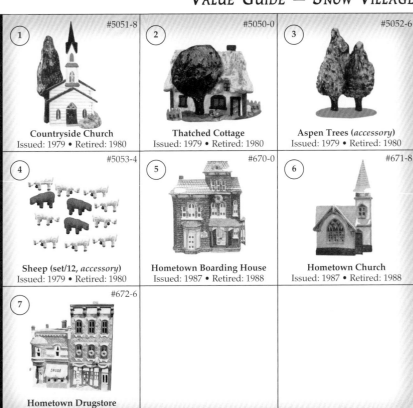

1 #5051-8
Countryside Church
Issued: 1979 • Retired: 1980

2 #5050-0
Thatched Cottage
Issued: 1979 • Retired: 1980

3 #5052-6
Aspen Trees (*accessory*)
Issued: 1979 • Retired: 1980

4 #5053-4
Sheep (set/12, *accessory*)
Issued: 1979 • Retired: 1980

5 #670-0
Hometown Boarding House
Issued: 1987 • Retired: 1988

6 #671-8
Hometown Church
Issued: 1987 • Retired: 1988

7 #672-6
Hometown Drugstore
Issued: 1988 • Retired: 1989

MEADOWLAND †	Original Price	Status	Market Value	Year Purch.	Price Paid	Value of My Collection
1. Countryside Church	$25.00	Retired	$720.00			
2. Thatched Cottage	$30.00	Retired	$700.00			
3. Aspen Trees (accessory)	$16.00	Retired	$400.00			
4. Sheep (set/12, accessory)	$12.00	Retired	$300.00			
† springtime set, not officially part of Snow Village or Heritage Village						
BACHMAN'S HOMETOWN SERIES ‡						
5. Hometown Boarding House	$34.00	Retired	$320.00			
6. Hometown Church	$40.00	Retired	$350.00			
7. Hometown Drug Store	$40.00	Retired	$585.00			
‡ available at Bachman's in Minnesota, not officially part of Snow Village or Heritage Village						

✎ **PENCIL TOTALS**

	PRICE PAID	MARKET VALUE

MEADOWLAND/BACHMAN'S

143

Use this page to record future Snow Village accessories.

ACCESSORIES SNOW VILLAGE	Original Price	Status	Market Value	Year Purch.	Price Paid	Value of My Collection
PENCIL TOTALS					PRICE PAID	MARKET VALUE

Total Value Of My Collection

Record the value of your collection here by adding the pencil totals from the bottom of each value guide page.

SNOW VILLAGE	Price Paid	Market Value
Page 103		
Page 104		
Page 105		
Page 106		
Page 107		
Page 108		
Page 109		
Page 110		
Page 111		
Page 112		
Page 113		
Page 114		
Page 115		
Page 116		
Page 117		
Page 118		
Page 119		
Page 120		
Page 121		
Page 122		
Page 123		
Page 124		
Page 125		
Page 126		
TOTAL		

ACCESSORIES SNOW VILLAGE	Price Paid	Market Value
Page 127		
Page 128		
Page 129		
Page 130		
Page 131		
Page 132		
Page 133		
Page 135		
Page 136		
Page 137		
Page 138		
Page 139		
Page 140		
Page 141		
Page 142		
Page 144		
TOTAL		

MEADOWLAND/BACHMAN'S	Price Paid	Market Value
Page 143		
TOTAL		

GRAND TOTALS	PRICE PAID	MARKET VALUE

COLLECTOR'S
VALUE GUIDE™

Secondary Market Overview

As with most collectible lines, the Department 56 secondary market begins when pieces are removed from production and are no longer available from retailers. Department 56 retires pieces every year, at which point a mad scramble ensues as collectors try to add these pieces to their collections before they "disappear" from stores. Once this happens, collectors must find other ways of acquiring the pieces they never had the chance to purchase – they must look on the secondary market.

1. Where is the secondary market?

There are various ways in which collectors can buy and sell pieces on the secondary market. The first step is to check with your retailer, as many retailers act as middlemen or have connections with other collectors. The easiest and most direct way to reach other collectors is through a *secondary market exchange service*. Collectors list the pieces they wish to sell or buy with the exchange service, which publishes a list of the pieces and the asking price. The exchange acts as the middleman in the transaction for a commission for each completed sale (usually between 10% and 20%). One benefit of using an exchange service is that you can reach collectors all over the country with minimal work. Most exchange listings are published monthly and may require a subscription or membership fee. A few generate daily listings which collectors can call for and receive by mail. A typical secondary market listing could read: "Ivy Glen Church, 71/2, 74/3, 77/1," which translates to two sellers asking for $71, three asking $74, etc. There also are exchange services that sell *their own* pieces and not those of collectors; there would be no commission in these cases. On page 149 is a listing of some secondary market exchange services and newsletters that deal with Department 56 collectibles.

Many newsletters and magazines feature their own "swap & sell" sections, which operate much the same way as the exchange services. Some collectors place *classified advertisements* in their local newspapers (under Antiques/Collectibles), but it may take longer to sell pieces this way because newspapers reach a general readership and not collectors specifically. The newest secondary market source is the *Internet*.

COLLECTOR'S
VALUE GUIDE™

Secondary Market Overview

More and more collectors are making use of on-line price listings, which have the virtue of being updated immediately. Department 56 now has its own web site (*www.dept56.com*) which is a good source for general information but does not deal with the secondary market.

Some *retailers* are also active on the secondary market, either working as an exchange service or selling directly to collectors. If a collector is looking to sell a large number of pieces or an entire collection, contacting a retailer may be ideal because of the dollar amounts involved. Other retailers who don't buy and sell secondary market pieces may sponsor *secondary market collector shows* as a service to their customers. Local and regional collector clubs also sponsor secondary market events.

2. How does the secondary market work?

Usually the value of a piece will rise quickly after its retirement has been announced by Department 56. Limited editions, signed pieces and special event pieces frequently command the highest prices on the secondary market. Not all limited editions are highly coveted; it all depends on how many pieces were made, how much it costs and of course, how popular it is with collectors. The same goes for open stock pieces that are retired. As a general rule, prices tend to increase over the years as fewer pieces are available on the secondary market. Pieces produced for only two or three years will typically have a higher secondary market value than those in production for a greater number of years.

No matter how old or rare a piece is, it will always be less valuable if it has been damaged. Many secondary market listings use notations such as "factory flaw" or "chipped," conditions which will decrease the value of a piece on the secondary market. Sometimes pieces suffer damage in the course of being displayed; common blemishes include stray wisps of paint, water damage, scrapes and chips. Remember to inspect your pieces carefully whether you're buying or selling. Be aware that some pieces on the secondary market have been repaired or restored. There's nothing wrong with buying a restored piece, so long as you know that it has been repaired and you understand that its resale value will decrease. Expect to pay less for a restored piece on the secondary market.

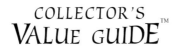
COLLECTOR'S
VALUE GUIDE™

Secondary Market Overview

Collectors should beware of rumors. Take the case of "Palace Theatre" from *Christmas in the City*, which was introduced in 1987 and retired in 1989. It was a large piece and had experienced many production problems. Sometime in 1990 rumors began to spread that a large number of pieces were broken during shipment and soon the story was that a whole shipment had been lost at sea. Prices rose rapidly as collectors scrambled to find what they thought would be a rare commodity. The secondary market value remains high today even though many dealers now feel there was no basis in fact to the story.

Variations of a particular piece can be another factor which may affect the secondary market value. While many of these variations are incidental changes due to the production process, other variations are extremely rare and can add to the secondary market value of a piece.

Another often-overlooked factor in the value of your collectibles is packaging. In the "real world," a box is just a box; but in the world of collectibles, boxes and packing sleeves take on an important new meaning. First, they are the best way to protect your pieces when they aren't out on display. Boxes also affect the secondary market value of your pieces. Those sold without boxes or with damaged boxes generally command a lower price, as many collectors feel a piece is somehow "incomplete" without its box.

Sales on the secondary market typically slow down in the summer and pick up as the holidays approach, although more and more the Department 56 villages are becoming a year-round hobby. Because demand for retired pieces increases later in the year, prices generally increase as well, so you may prefer to sell late in the year and buy earlier in the year. There really is no "right" or "wrong" time to buy or sell; it all depends on how much you're willing to pay for a piece you want to add to your display or how much it will take for you to part with one of your buildings.

Lastly, it's important to remember that not every retired building will soar in value, so if your sole reason to collect is for the investment, you may be disappointed. You're much better off doing it for the fun!

COLLECTOR'S
VALUE GUIDE™

Secondary Market Overview

EXCHANGES & NEWSLETTERS

56 Directions
Jeff & Susan McDermott
364 Spring Street Ext.
Glastonbury, CT 06033
(203) 633-8192

Collectible Exchange, Inc.
6621 Columbiana Road
New Middletown, OH 44442
(216) 542-9646

The Cottage Locator
Frank and Florence Wilson
211 No. Bridebrook Rd.
East Lyme, CT 06333
(860) 739-0705

Dickens' Exchange
Lynda W. Blankenship
5150 Highway 22, Suite C-9
Mandeville, LA 70471
(504) 845-1954

Martha's Exchange Service
3961 Kiawa Drive
Orlando, FL 32837
(407) 438-4869

New England Collectibles Exchange
Bob Dorman
201 Pine Avenue
Clarksburg, MA 01247
1-800-854-6323

Roger's Collectors' Marketplace
Roger Poole
8017 N. Hughes Drive
Spokane, WA 99208
(509) 467-2300

The Village Chronicle
Peter and Jeanne George
200 Post Road, Box 311
Warwick, RI 02888
(401) 467-9343

The Village Press
Roger Bain
P.O. Box 556
Rockford, IL 61105
(815) 965-0901

Villages Classified
Paul and Mirta Burns
P.O. Box 34166
Granada Hills, CA 91394-9166
(818) 368-6765

What The Dickens
Judith Isaacson
2885 West Ribera Place
Tucson, AZ 85742
(602) 297-7019

Variations

Although Department 56 collectibles are produced from master molds, the buildings can have variations which may or may not affect their secondary market value. Variations sometimes occur because the pieces are finished and painted by hand, and because of the firing process in which the paint is fused to the porcelain. Common variations include slight changes in height, color tone or even misspellings of names on the buildings or on the bottoms of pieces. While not every variation affects the secondary market value of a piece, there are some variations that are important enough to capture the attention of collectors. The following is a listing of the known variations that affect the secondary market value of Heritage Village and Snow Village buildings. See Value Guide section for price variations.

* * *

DICKENS' VILLAGE

Blythe Pond Mill House (#6508-0)
The name is misspelled on the bottom of many pieces, reading "By The Pond." In this instance, the misspelled version is more common than the correct version.

Dickens' Village Church (#6516-1)
The church can be found in five different colors (listed from earliest to latest): white, yellow or cream, green, tan, dark/butterscotch.

Nicholas Nickleby Cottage (#5925-0)
Early pieces had a spelling error on the bottom of the pieces, "Nickolas Nickleby." The misspelling was quickly corrected on later pieces.

Peggotty's Seaside Cottage (#5550-6)
This building, shaped like an overturned boat, was unpainted on the first pieces which resulted in a tan or white appearance. Later pieces were painted a dark green.

* * *

NEW ENGLAND VILLAGE

Ada's Bed And Boarding House (#5940-4)
This piece has three variations. The first is lemon yellow and the rear steps are part of the building's mold. The second piece is a paler yellow and the rear steps are also part of the building's mold. The third piece is also a pale yellow, but the rear steps are added on to the building from a separate mold.

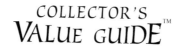

COLLECTOR'S
VALUE GUIDE™

Berkshire House (#5942-0)
The original version is blue with cream shutters and has a light gray porch, while the later version is teal with tan shutters and has a dark gray porch and steps.

Steeple Church (#6530-7)
The church from the original "New England Village" set features a tree that was attached with a porcelain slip or with glue. The seam on the porcelain slip version was cleaner, but not as strong as the seam on the glued-on version.

❋ ❋ ❋

ALPINE VILLAGE

Alpine Church (#6541-2)
The first church had white trim and is very rare while the later and more common versions have tan or caramel-colored trim.

❋ ❋ ❋

GENERAL HERITAGE VILLAGE ACCESSORIES

Village Express Van (#5865-3)
The regular "Village Express Van" is green and was available at all retailers before being retired in 1996. Many special vans have been introduced, including a black van, a gold van, a Canadian van and more than a dozen that were produced for individual stores.

❋ ❋ ❋

DICKENS' VILLAGE ACCESSORIES

Carolers (set/3, #6526-9)
The first set of carolers can be identified by the white lamp post and little detail on the carolers' faces. The second set has a black lamp post and the girl and woman have blonde hair. The third set also has a black lamp post, but is larger than the first two and the girl and woman have brown hair.

Dover Coach (#6590-0)
In the original piece, the coachman has no mustache, while in later versions he has a mustache.

Ox Sled (#5951-0)
In the first version, the driver is wearing tan pants and sits on a green seat cushion. In the second version, the driver is wearing blue pants, sits on a black seat cushion and the oxen and cart are larger.

❋ ❋ ❋

NEW ENGLAND VILLAGE ACCESSORIES

Amish Family (set/3, #5948-0)
The father in the original piece had a mustache, but because Amish men do not wear mustaches, later versions had no mustache.

Variations

Harvest Pumpkin Wagon (#56591)
This piece comes from the same mold as a special anniversary piece for Bachman's called "Horse-Drawn Squash Cart," the difference being that one wagon carries pumpkins and the other, squash.

✳ ✳ ✳

SNOW VILLAGE

General Store (#5012-0)
The earliest version of this piece is white, but there also are tan and gold versions. On some pieces, the sign reads "Y & L Brothers" or "S & L Brothers."

Knob Hill (#5055-9)
The earlier pieces are gray and later pieces are bright yellow.

Small Double Trees (#5016-1)
The first version has blue birds sitting on the branches and later versions have red birds.

Train Station With 3 Train Cars (set/4, #5085-6)
The original station is smaller, has six window panes, a round window in the door and brick on the front. The later, larger version has eight window panes, two square windows in the door and brick on the front and the sides.

✳ ✳ ✳

SNOW VILLAGE ACCESSORIES

For Sale Sign (#5108-0)
A promotional blank sign (#581-9) was available at retailers belonging to the Gift Creations Concepts buying group in 1989.

For Sale Sign (#5166-7)
Special version produced for 1990 Bachman's Village Gathering (#539-8).

Here Comes Santa (various)
Twenty-four different versions of this piece were available only at selected retailers in 1996.

Kids Around The Tree (#5094-6)
The early pieces are much larger than later versions.

A Visit With Santa (various)
Eight versions of this piece (personalized for individual stores) were released in 1995.

Water Tower (#5133-0)
A rare variation reads "Moline, Home of John Deere" and was available only through John Deere.

✳ ✳ ✳

Insurance Coverage for Collectibles

While the pieces in your collection hold sentimental value, they also have a dollar value. When you add up each purchase, you may find that you've invested quite a bit putting your collection together. Then, when you look at the secondary market values and figure out what it would cost to replace pieces in your collection, you might decide you want to insure your collection just as you insure the other valuables in your home. There are three steps to determining whether you should insure your collection; *knowing your coverage, documenting the contents and value of your collection* and *weighing the risk.*

1. Know your coverage

Collectibles are considered part of the contents of a house and as such, they are typically included in homeowners or renters insurance policies. Ask your agent about the types of loss or damage your policy covers and what it doesn't cover. A standard policy covers household contents for damage or loss from perils such as fire, hurricanes and theft. Common exclusions include earthquakes, floods and breakage through routine handling. In addition to determining the types of loss that are covered, ask your agent about the dollar value that would be paid out in the event that you have to file a claim. The amount paid out will vary based on the type of coverage you have. Today, most insurance policies are written at replacement value which would provide enough money to replace a lost or damaged collection. Replacement value policies pay out the amount needed to actually replace the items. This is especially important for collectibles because they appreciate in value.

2. Document the contents and value of your collection

In order to determine how much coverage you need, you must first document your collection to calculate how much it would cost to replace your pieces. There are many ways to document your collection, from a simple listing to hiring an appraiser; but you should check with your insurance agent first to find out what records the insurance company will

Insuring Your Collection

accept in the event of a loss. Generally companies want to see proof that you own particular pieces and proof of their value.

Two of the best forms of documentation are receipts and a "schedule" or listing of each piece in your collection, including the purchase date, price paid, where you purchased the piece, special markings and current value on the secondary market. Some companies will accept a reputable secondary market guide, such as the Collector's Value Guide, for pricing. The *Value Guide* section includes 1997 secondary market prices to help you determine the replacement value of your retired collectibles. Keep in mind that your insurance carrier may want to distinguish between items which are available through normal retail outlets versus pieces which are no longer available (retired, suspended, etc.). It makes sense to list or "schedule" your valuable retired pieces on your policy, just as you would for jewelry and other important valuables.

If you have particularly valuable pieces or if you have an extensive collection, you should note that the more valuable the item, the more demanding the insurance company will be for industry-accepted valuation. They may even want a professional appraisal. For appraisers in your area, contact the American Society of Appraisers at 1-800-ASA-VALU. The Society was established in 1936 and counts 6,500 members from 82 chapters across the United States and around the world.

Photographs and video footage of your collection are a good back-up in case of an unforeseen problem claim. Snapshots and video should record closeup views of the piece (including the bottoms) and show any registration marks, edition numbers or artist signatures. Print two sets of photographs; store one set in your home and give the second set to a friend or put it in a safe deposit box.

COLLECTOR'S
VALUE GUIDE™

3. Weigh the risk

After you calculate the replacement cost of your collection, you can then determine if you have adequate insurance to cover any losses. To do this, add the estimated value of your home furnishings to the value of your collectibles (as totaled in this book) and consult your insurance policy for the amount of coverage. Compare the total value of the contents of your home to the dollar amount you would be paid in the event that you had to file a claim.

After you compare numbers, if you find your insurance policy does not provide enough coverage, you could purchase additional insurance for your collectibles. This can be done by adding a "Personal Articles Floater" (PAF) or a "Fine Arts Floater" or "rider" to your homeowners policy which provides broader coverage and insures your collection for specific dollar amounts.

Another option is to purchase a separate policy specifically for collectibles from a specialized insurance provider. One such company is American Collectors Insurance, Inc. in Cherry Hill, New Jersey, which offers coverage for a wide variety of collectibles, from figurines to dolls to memorabilia. A sample application form is shown here. You can reach American Collectors Insurance at: 1-800-257-5758.

As with all insurance, you must weigh the risk of loss against the cost of additional coverage.

Apply Now For A Collectibles Insurance Policy

COLLECTIBLES INSURANCE POLICY APPLICATION

Underwritten by American Bankers Insurance Company of Florida

sample application

Collectors' Corner

Department 56 Biography

Originally, Department 56 was part of Bachman's, a large retail floral and garden center in Minnesota which listed its departments by number. Department "56" was the number assigned to its wholesale gift imports division. Department 56 was established as an independent company in 1976 and was incorporated in 1984.

Inspired by a holiday trip with friends to a quaint little town along the St. Croix River in Minnesota, company president Ed Bazinet introduced a line of four lighted houses and two churches. The line, named The Original Snow Village, started a phenomenon and Department 56 introduced more buildings each subsequent year. In order to keep the line at a reasonable size, the company retired several pieces in 1979 and ushered in the era of the Department 56 secondary market.

Based on the success of The Original Snow Village, Department 56 created a second line called *Dickens' Village* in 1984. This new series was very different in theme from Snow Village, as it was inspired by the traditional Victorian Christmas immortalized by Charles Dickens' literary classic *A Christmas Carol*. Within two years, the company added more themed villages and grouped them under The Heritage Village Collection. In addition to the villages, Department 56 also produces other collectible lines such as Snowbabies, Winter Silhouette and more.

In 1992, Department 56 was bought by Forstmann Little, a New York investment firm, and a year later, the company debuted on the New York Stock Exchange as "Dept56." Recent changes for Department 56 include the 1996 appointment of Susan Engel as CEO and the presence of Department 56 on the Internet (visit their site on the World Wide Web at *www.dept56.com*). Today, Department 56 enjoys over $185 million in sales, with villages accounting for over two-thirds of the total. Department 56 has earned numerous industry awards and commendations for its high-quality collectibles.

> *Department 56 opens up its showroom to the public on Friday afternoons during the summer months. For information and reservations, please write or call:*
>
> Department 56
> One Village Place Showroom Tour
> 6436 City West Parkway
> Eden Prairie, MN 55344
> 1-800-LIT-TOWN

COLLECTOR'S
VALUE GUIDE™

Collectors' Corner

Production, Packaging And Pricing

Every great work of art starts with an idea. The artists at Department 56 spend many hours brainstorming to design the quaint little villages we've all grown to know and love. Once a concept is approved, scale drawings, similar to blueprints, must then be created. Artists sketch every detail, from windows to individual bricks. Sculptors in Taiwan and the Philippines then create a clay model based on the artist's rendition. The main body is created first with a 15% overscale to compensate for shrinkage that occurs during firing. Then, the exterior details such as porches, chimneys and towers are sculpted separately and added later. The bottom stamp is also prepared at this stage.

An impression is taken from the model using a fine plaster, which serves as the "mother mold." From this, "case" or production molds are developed from high density composite which is essential in preventing exterior details on the houses from wearing down after extended use of the mold. Next, during the casting process, liquid clay "slip" is poured into the mold and allowed to harden. The resulting clay structure is then sanded and the exterior features cemented to the main piece. Door and window openings are cut into the piece and it is allowed to dry. Later, the piece is kiln-fired at temperatures as high as 1250° F, resulting in a pure white, rock hard porcelain. Once the piece is cooled, artists hand-paint it; then it is fired again at a lower temperature to bond the paint to the surface. At this stage, the Snow Village pieces are covered with a clear glaze and fired again to create their glossy finish.

Each piece is carefully cleaned and placed in foam cartons (boxes) and a cardboard sleeve is slipped over the box. The names of the collection and the piece are printed on the sleeves. The box also has room for the electrical cord and light bulb, as well as detachable details (such as signs) that go with the piece.

Suggested retail prices for current buildings start around $30 and can go as high as $120, primarily for limited editions and multiple-piece sets. Porcelain accessories range from about $10 to $50, with several larger accessories and sets reaching $75.

COLLECTOR'S
VALUE GUIDE™

Collectors' Corner

Current Display Pieces

While there certainly are a wide variety of porcelain accessories to choose from, Department 56 also produces numerous display accessories that can be used to enhance your village. These include trees, which will add color and realism to your mountainside; benches and fences for your town square; and even snow, which is an essential part of every display.

Below is a list of the current display accessories, which are available at most retailers. Most of these accessories can be used for both Heritage Village and Snow Village, while a few are designed for a specific village and these are identified as (HV) or (SV). The new issues for 1997 are marked with an asterisk (*). Several accessories are pictured so you can decide just which style of tree or fence will fit best into your display.

SNOW
1. Blanket Of New Fallen Snow   4995-6
2. Fresh Fallen Snow   49979
   (7-oz. bag)
3. Fresh Fallen Snow   49980
   (2-lb. box)
4. Real Plastic Snow   4998-1
   (7-oz. bag)
5. Real Plastic Snow   4999-9
   (2-lb. box)

FENCES
1. Chain Link Fence (set/3)   5234-5
2. Chain Link Fence   5235-3
   Extensions (set/4)
3. Courtyard Fence w/Steps (HV) 5220-5
4. Fence Extension (set/9) (HV) 5515-8
5. Frosty Tree-Lined Picket   5207-8
   Fence (SV)
6. Snow Fence (flexible,   5204-3
   wood) (SV)

7. Split Rail Fence (set/4)   52597
8. Tree-Lined Courtyard   5212-4
   Fence (HV)
9. Twig Snow Fence   52598
10. White Picket Fence (SV)   5100-4
11. White Picket Fence (set/4)   5101-2
    (SV)
12. White Picket Fence   52625*
    Extensions (set/6)
13. White Picket Fence   52624*
    with Gate (set/5)
14. Wrought Iron Fence   5998-6
    (2 Asst.) (HV)
15. Wrought Iron Fence   5999-4
    (set/4) (HV)
16. Wrought Iron Fence   5253-1
    Extension (metal)
17. Wrought Iron Fence   5252-3
    w/Gate (set/5)
18. Wrought Iron Gate w/Fence 5514-0
    (set/9) (HV)

White Picket Fence With Gate

White Picket Fence Extensions

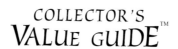

TREES

1. Arctic Pines (set/3) — 52608
2. Autumn Maple Tree — 5254-0
3. Autumn Trees (set/3) — 52616
4. Bare Branch Tree w/25 Lights — 5243-4
5. Bare Branch Trees (set/6) — 52623*
6. Cedar Forest (set/3) — 52606
7. Evergreen Trees (set/3) — 5205-1
8. Frosted Fir Tree (set/4) — 52605
9. Frosted Hemlock (Set/2) — 52638*
10. Frosted Norway Pines (set/3) — 5175-6
11. Frosted Spruce (Set/2) — 52637*
12. Frosted Topiary Cones (set/2) — 5200-0
13. Frosted Topiary Cones (set/4) — 5201-9
14. Frosted Topiary Cones (set/8, Asst. Lg.) — 5202-7
15. Frosted Topiary Cones (set/8, Asst. Sm.) — 5203-5
16. Jack Pines (set/3) — 52622*
17. Pencil Pines (set/3) — 5246-9
18. Pole Pine Forest (set/5) — 5527-1
19. Pole Pine Tree, Lg. — 5529-8
20. Pole Pine Tree, Sm. — 5528-0
21. Ponderosa Pines (set/3) — 52607
22. Snowcapped Trees (set/2) — 52604
23. Snowy Evergreen Trees, Lg. (set/5) — 52614
24. Snowy Evergreen Trees, Med. (set/6) — 52613
25. Snowy Evergreen Trees, Sm. (set/6) — 52612
26. Snowy Scotch Pines (set/3) — 52615
27. Village Birch Tree Cluster — 52631*
28. Village Double Pine Trees — 52619
29. Village Holly Tree — 52630*
30. Village Towering Pines (set/2) — 52632*
31. Wagon Wheel Pine Grove — 52617
32. Winter Birch (set/6) — 52636*

Village Birch Tree Cluster

Village Holly Tree

MISCELLANEOUS ACCENT PIECES

1. Acrylic Icicles (set/4) — 5211-6
2. Boulevard Lampposts (set/4) — 52627*
3. Brick Road (set/2) — 5210-8
4. Brick Town Square — 52601
5. Christmas Eave Trim — 5511-5
6. Christmas In The City Subway Entrance (metal) (HV) — 5541-7
7. Cobblestone Road (set/2) — 5984-6
8. Cobblestone Town Square — 52602
9. Coca-Cola Neon Sign (SV) — 5482-8
10. Country Road Lampposts (set/2) — 52628*
11. Election Yard Signs (set/6) — 52599
12. Fallen Leaves (3-oz. bag) — 52610
13. Flexible Sisal Hedge (set/3) — 52596
14. Hybrid Landscape (set/22) — 52600
15. It's A Grand Old Flag (SV) — 5417-8
16. Let It Snow Snowman Sign — 52594
17. Mill Creek Bridge — 52635*
18. Mill Creek, Curved Section — 52634*
19. Mill Creek, Straight Section — 52633*
20. Mountain Centerpiece — 52643*
21. Pink Flamingos (set/4) — 52595
22. Railroad Crossing Sign (battery, set/2) — 5501-8
23. Revolving Display Stand — 52640*
24. Sisal Wreath (set/6) (SV) — 5419-4
25. Sled & Skis (set/2) — 5233-7
26. Tacky Wax — 5217-5

COLLECTOR'S
VALUE GUIDE™

Collectors' Corner

MISC. ACCENT PIECES, cont.

27. Town Clock (2 Asst., metal) 5110-1
28. Village Landscape (set/14) 52590
29. Village Magic Smoke
    (6 oz. bottle) 52620
30. Village Mountain Backdrop 5257-4
    (set/2)
31. Village Mountain Tunnel 52582
32. Village Mountain w/ Frosted 5228-0
    Sisal Trees, Lg. (set/14)
33. Village Mountain w/ Frosted 5227-2
    Sisal Trees, Med. (set/8)
34. Village Mountain w/ Frosted 5226-4
    Sisal Trees, Sm. (set/5)
35. Village Mylar Skating Pond 5208-6
    (set/2)
36. Village Pine Point Pond 52618
37. Village Snow Machine
    w/Snow 52592
38. Village Square Clock Tower 52591
39. Village Stone Wall 52629*
40. Wrought Iron Park Bench 5230-2

Mill Creek Bridge

ELECTRICAL

1. 6-Socket Light Set 9927-9
2. AC/DC Adapter 5502-6
3. Lights Mini Light 5215-9
   (set/14)
4. Multi Outlet Plug Strip 9933-3
5. Replacement Light Bulb (set/3) 9924-4
6. Revolving Tree 52603
7. Single Cord Set w/Light 9902-8
8. Town Tree w/50 LED Lights 52639*
9. Traffic Light (set/2) (SV) 5500-0
10. Turn Of The Century 5504-2
    Lamppost (set/4) (SV)
11. Utility (set/8, metal) 5512-3
    (2 stop signs, 4 parking
    meters, 2 traffic lights) (HV)
12. Village 20 Bulb Strand 99278*
13. Village LED Light Bulb 99247*
14. Village Mini Lights 52626*
15. Village Spotlight (set/2) 52611
16. Village Spotlight
    Replacement Bulbs (set/6) 99246*

LAMPS

1. Double Street Lamps 5996-0
   (battery, set/4) (HV)
2. Street Lamps 3636-6
   (battery, set/6) (HV)

VILLAGE BRITE LITES

1. Adapter 5225-6
2. Brite Lites, Red (set/20) 5245-0
3. "Department 56" 9846-9
4. Fence (set/4) 5236-1
5. "I Love My Village" 5222-1
6. "Merry Christmas" 5223-0
7. Reindeer, Flashing 5224-8
8. Santa Waving 5239-6
9. Snowman 5237-0
10. Tree w/Flashing Star 5238-8
11. Waving Flag 5244-2

COLLECTOR'S
VALUE GUIDE™

Collectors' Corner

Now That's The Way To Display

Whether you're a collector of one or a collector of many, you'll want to make your display as decorative as can be. Remember that there is always something to learn about displaying and that there are many different ways to make a mountain, bridge or pond accentuate the pieces in your collection. Also remember that creating a display can be kept simple, solely by creating different elevations with your pieces. You can experiment any way you like by being as elaborate or as simple as you choose – after all, that's the fun of displaying! Listed below are a variety of tips to help you with your Department 56 display.

Begin with supplies . . .

Before you get started, you should have some basic display tools, including foam board, a hot glue gun, tacky wax, paint and props like plastic snow, snow blankets, rocks, moss and twigs. This way, should you decide to do an elaborate display, you will have all the props you'll need before you begin.

Create a base . . .

You may opt to create a platform to support your collection so you can transport your display from one place to another. If so, begin with a piece of 1 to 2 inch insulation board. Lay out the basic design of the village and draw a pencil outline of each building. This way you will have an accurate base to build around. Add height by stacking the foam, then trim the sides to add contour. Always trim on an angle to assure smoothness and a more natural finish. You can push toothpicks up through the base to secure fences and other accessories.

Determine a setting . . .

There are many places to feature your collection within your home that will help accentuate it. For instance, mantels always make an excellent showcase and if you need additional space, why not build a shelf overhead? Placing your pieces under the Christmas tree is another good idea as the tree branches will serve as decorative trim.

COLLECTOR'S ™
VALUE GUIDE

Collectors' Corner

Other suggestions include creating a centerpiece on the dining room table or presenting your collection inside a bookcase or bay window (the frosty windowpanes make a picturesque backdrop). Wherever you choose to create your *Dickens' Village* display, remember that in 19th century London, buildings were close together. The same goes for today's bustling cities. Thus, placing many of your *Dickens' Village* and *Christmas in the City* pieces close together will add realism.

Landscaping and elevations . . .

Mountains are an excellent way to create depth and Department 56 offers them in three sizes, each including a set of sisal trees. Of course, you can always opt to create your own by cutting and trimming foam into different shapes. When using trees, do so liberally! Use different types for variety to create a park-like setting or group them together to create forest-like scenery. The bottoms of Department 56 trees are easy to remove so you can push them right into your base, which will give them stability as well as flexibility.

Waterworld . . .

Skating ponds are a fun part of every winter scene. To create your own, spray crystal frost on a mirror tile for a realistic look. For larger displays, the new "Village Waterfall" accessory from Department 56 could be an impressive addition.

Snowy surfaces . . .

What is a winter display without the white stuff? You can create different snow textures by either spreading out plastic snow evenly across your base for a "blanket" effect, or you can drift throughout your village display for that "fresh-fallen" look. Also, you can shape snow mounds by rounding contours into your foam base with a steel wire brush.

Remember, there is no "right" way to display your collection. The important thing is to use creativity and choose pieces and accessories that are most appealing to you or that rekindle a bit of nostalgia. Nothing touches the heart more than a collection filled with happy memories!

COLLECTOR'S
VALUE GUIDE™

Department 56 Collectors' Clubs

Although there is no official club sponsored by Department 56, many collectors have joined to form their own "local chapters" within their home states. During club meetings, members gather together to discuss many topics from new releases to display techniques to trading pieces amongst one another. This is also a good way to keep apprised of collector events and organize plans to attend them together. Ask your favorite retailer if there is a Department 56 collectors' club in your area. You may be surprised at how many people have caught the same "collecting bug."

In fact, the idea of the "local chapter" has become so popular that over 100 independent clubs across the country have joined to form the National Council of "56" Clubs. The council publishes its own newsletter, sponsors regional Department 56 events and facilitates communication between collectors and Department 56. You can also contact them if you wish to start up a club in your own area. Write to:

National Council of "56" Clubs
651 Perimeter Drive, Suite 600
Lexington, KY 40517

Department 56 maintains contact with collectors directly through its *Quarterly* publication. The *Quarterly* covers new releases, retirements and features on Department 56 lines. It also includes the "Dear Ms. Lit Town" column featuring answers to readers' questions by Judith Price, the director of consumer services. Collectors interested in subscribing to the *Quarterly* can write to Department 56 at P.O. Box 44056, Eden Prairie, MN 55344-1456 or call 1-800-LIT-TOWN.

COLLECTOR'S ™
VALUE GUIDE

Collectors' Corner

Address Book

Use this space to list your favorite retailers, fellow collectors, collectors clubs, secondary market dealers or anyone who is an important part of your collecting hobby.

Name _____

Address _____

_____

Phone _____

Notes _____

Name _____

Address _____

_____

Phone _____

Notes _____

Name _____

Address _____

_____

Phone _____

Notes _____

Name _____

Address _____

_____

Phone _____

Notes _____

COLLECTOR'S
VALUE GUIDE™

Collectors' Notebook

Name _____

Address _____

_____

Phone _____

Notes _____

Name _____

Address _____

_____

Phone _____

Notes _____

Name _____

Address _____

_____

Phone _____

Notes _____

Name _____

Address _____

_____

Phone _____

Notes _____

Name _____

Address _____

_____

Phone _____

Notes _____

COLLECTOR'S
VALUE GUIDE™

Collectors' Notebook

Monthly Planner

    This monthly planner is for your notes about store events, collector shows, club meetings, etc. in your area.

January — New Department 56 introductions are announced to retailers.

February — New pieces start to arrive at selected retail stores.

March

April

May — Mid-year introductions are announced to retailers.

June

COLLECTOR'S
VALUE GUIDE™

Collectors' Notebook

July

August

September

October

November   *Ask your retailer about retirements and Open House events.*

December

COLLECTOR'S
VALUE GUIDE™

Collectors' Notebook

Collector's Diary

This section is designed for you to write down important notes about your Department 56 collection.

Glossary

accessory—pieces designed to enhance the display of Heritage and Snow Village buildings. Accessories are typically non-lit miniature figurines depicting townspeople, vehicles, landscape items such as trees or snow, and more.

animated—a piece with motion. Department 56 has issued several animated pieces in recent years, including three for 1997 (a ski mountain, a waterfall and an accessory track).

bottomstamp—also called an "understamp," these are identifying marks on the underside of a figurine or building. Heritage Village pieces have a bottomstamp which includes the series name (*Dickens', Alpine,* etc.), the title of the piece, the copyright date and the Department 56 logo.

building—general term for miniature lighted shops, offices, homes, churches, etc.

catalog exclusives—Department 56 has offered early releases of several "next year's introductions" to a group of retailers who participate in a single specific selected gift catalog. During the introduction year, these pieces are usually available to Showcase Dealers as well.

Charles Dickens' Signature Series©—This Heritage Village series is produced under a licensing arrangement with the Charles Dickens Heritage Limited Foundation, which donates the royalties from the Signature Series to charitable projects in England and the United States. These buildings have been limited to one year of production. This year's release, "Gad's Hill Place," will be the last piece in this series.

collectibles—anything and everything that is "able to be collected," whether it's figurines, dolls...or even *thimbles* can be considered a "collectible," but it is generally recognized that a true collectible should be something that increases in value over time.

Gift Creations Concepts (GCC)—a syndicated catalog group of over 300 retail stores nationwide.

Gold Key Dealers—Showcase retailers who are recognized for outstanding commitment to the Department 56 product line. This is the highest distinction a retailer can achieve.

history list—Department 56 brochures for Heritage Village and Snow Village which list the item number, title, issue year, suggested retail price and retirement year.

COLLECTOR'S
VALUE GUIDE™

Glossary

International Collectible Exposition—national collectible shows held in Rosemont, Illinois each June or July (formerly held in South Bend, Indiana) and in April alternating between Secaucus, New Jersey one year and Long Beach, California the next.

issue date—for Department 56 pieces, the year of production is considered the year of "issue," although the piece may not become available to collectors until the following year.

issue price—the suggested retail price of an item when it is first introduced.

limited edition (LE)—a piece scheduled for a predetermined production quantity or time period. Some Heritage Village pieces have been limited to a specific number of pieces (ex. "Dickens' Village Mill" was limited to 2,500 pieces) or limited by year of production (ex. "Gad's Hill Place" is limited to 1997 production).

markings—any of the various identifying features found on a collectible. It can be information found on bottomstamps or backstamps, an artist's signature on the piece or even a symbol denoting a specific year or artist.

mid-year introductions—additional Department 56 pieces are announced in May, which is a follow-up to the major January introductions. These pieces are usually available in smaller allocations than "new" introductions during this first year, but become readily available in subsequent years.

mint condition—piece offered for sale on the secondary market that is in like-new condition. Mint-in-box means the piece is still in its original box.

N.A.L.E.D.—National Association of Limited Edition Dealers, a retail store buying group.

new introductions—new pieces in Heritage and Snow Villages which are announced in January.

open edition—a piece with no predetermined limitation on time or size of production run.

porcelain—the hard and non-absorbent material used to make Department 56 buildings; a kind of ceramic made primarily with kaolin (a pure form of clay) that is fired at temperatures approaching 1,450°C or 2,650° F.

Glossary

primary market—the conventional collectibles purchasing process in which collectors buy directly from dealers at issue price.

real estate—colloquial term for the subsegment of the collectibles industry that features small-scale buildings, cottages and villages.

release date—the year a piece becomes available to collectors. For most pieces, the release date is the year following the issue date.

retired—a piece which is taken out of production, never to be made again, usually followed by a scarcity of the piece and a rise in value on the secondary market (see definition for *secondary market*).

secondary market—the source for buying and selling collectibles according to basic supply-and-demand principles ("pay what the market will bear"). Popular pieces which have retired or have low production quantities can appreciate in value far above the original retail issue price. Pieces are sold through local and national newspaper ads, collector newsletters and through swap & sells at collector meetings.

series—special group within a collection based on a certain theme, such as the *American Architecture Series* in Snow Village.

Showcase Dealers—Department 56 has selected a group of retailers to be Showcase Dealers. Early shipments of new and limited edition pieces and a general, strong retail display supported with good inventory are features of many Showcase Dealers.

sleeve—thin cardboard cover that slips over a Styrofoam box, usually illustrated with information such as the name of the collection, name of the piece and black and white photograph of the piece.

swap & sell—collectors meet to buy, sell or trade items with each other.

Alphabetical Index

– Key –

Pieces from Snow Village and Heritage Village are listed together in alphabetical order. The first page number refers to the piece's location within the Value Guide section and the second to the box in which it is pictured on that page.

COLLECTOR'S
VALUE GUIDE™

Alphabetical Index

COLLECTOR'S
VALUE GUIDE™

COLLECTOR'S
VALUE GUIDE™

Alphabetical Index

COLLECTOR'S
VALUE GUIDE™

Alphabetical Index

COLLECTOR'S
VALUE GUIDE™

Alphabetical Index

Alphabetical Index

COLLECTOR'S
VALUE GUIDE™

Alphabetical Index

COLLECTOR'S
VALUE GUIDE™

Alphabetical Index

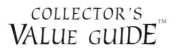

Alphabetical Index

COLLECTOR'S
VALUE GUIDE™

COLLECTOR'S
VALUE GUIDE™

Numerical Index

COLLECTOR'S
VALUE GUIDE™

Numerical Index

COLLECTOR'S
VALUE GUIDE™

Numerical Index

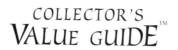

Numerical Index

COLLECTOR'S
VALUE GUIDE™

Numerical Index

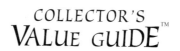

COLLECTOR'S
VALUE GUIDE™

Numerical Index

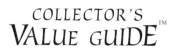

COLLECTOR'S
VALUE GUIDE™

Notes